Introduction

The Essentials of AQA GCSE French is meticulously matched to AQA GCSE French Specification A (3651) and Specification B (3652). Everything you need to know is contained within this book but, just as importantly, there is no superfluous material.

Written by Steve Harrison, a Principal Examiner with over 20 years' teaching experience, this revision guide is utterly reliable and extremely user-friendly, with information presented in small, relevant chunks that are easy to understand and absorb.

The guide is divided into four main sections that correspond with the 'Themes' on the course specification. Each section (or theme) covers five key topics. All the vocabulary and grammar needed to understand, speak and write about a topic can be found on those pages, supported by useful phrases, model answers and helpful hints. Tasks are included to reinforce what you have learned along with self-testing exercises.

The additional grammar and vocabulary at the back of the book is not specific to any one theme but will help to improve your overall understanding and use of the French language. This material is not optional - it could easily come up in a test.

An advisory section is also included, providing expert guidance on how best to prepare for your reading, writing, listening and speaking tests and ensure you achieve your full potential.

No reference is made to the different tiers in this guide because the content of the specification is exactly the same for all students. Consequently, some questions will be the same on both the foundation and higher test papers for reading, listening and writing. Only higher level students, however, are expected to be able to use some of the more advanced grammar and vocabulary in writing and speaking tests.

Regardless of your tier, you must be able to use three time frames (past, present and future) if you want to achieve a C grade or above and it is beneficial to cover as much material as possible in your revision. The main challenge for higher tier students is to expand, develop and justify their answers and to be able to identify attitudes and emotions. The practice questions in this guide will help you to do this.

Contents

Les saisons / The seasons

le printemps	spring
l'été	summer
l'automne	autumn
l'hiver	winter
en été	in summer
en automne	in autumn
en hiver	in winter
but au printemps	in spring

Les jours de la semaine / Days of the week

lundi	Monday
mardi	Tuesday
mercredi	Wednesday
jeudi	Thursday
vendredi	Friday
samedi	Saturday
dimanche	Sunday

Les mois de l'année / Months of the year

janvier	January
février	February
mars	March
avril	April
mai	May
juin	June
juillet	July
août	August
septembre	September
octobre	October
novembre	November
décembre	December

La date / The date

le quatorze janvier	14th January
le vingt-six mars	26th March
but le premier août	1st August

Les nombres / Numbers

0	zéro	29	vingt-neuf
1	un	30	trente
2	deux	31	trente et un
3	trois	40	quarante
4	quatre	50	cinquante
5	cinq	60	soixante
6	six	70	soixante-dix
7	sept	71	soixante et onze
8	huit	72	soixante-douze
9	neuf	73	soixante-treize
10	dix	79	soixante-dix-neuf
11	onze	80	quatre-vingts
12	douze	81	quatre-vingt-un
13	treize	90	quatre-vingt-dix
14	quatorze	91	quatre-vingt-onze
15	quinze	99	quatre-vingt-dix-neuf
16	seize	100	cent
17	dix-sept	101	cent un
18	dix-huit	110	cent dix
19	dix-neuf	200	deux cents
20	vingt	201	deux cent un
21	vingt et un	221	deux cent vingt et un
22	vingt-deux	1 000	mille
23	vingt-trois	1 200	mille deux cents
24	vingt-quatre	1 202	mille deux cent deux
25	vingt-cinq	2 000	deux mille
26	vingt-six	1 000 000	un million
27	vingt-sept	1 000 000 000	un milliard
28	vingt-huit		

 Helpful Hint

To change a number into a position e.g. 2nd, 3rd, 4th, you add **-ième** to the end. If the number ends in an **-e** (e.g. **quatre**), you need to take the **-e** off before adding the ending.

deux**ième**	second
trois**ième**	third
quatr**ième**	fourth

The exception to this rule is **un** (one):

premier / première   first

 Helpful Hint

In French, both weekdays and months of the year start with a lower case letter (not a Capital letter).

Make a note of the following uses:

mercredi	Wednesday / *on* Wednesday
le mercredi	*on* Wednesdays
en janvier / au mois de janvier	*in* January

The Essentials

L'alphabet/The alphabet

A	as in c<u>a</u>t
B	bay
C	say
D	day
E	as in <u>ugh</u>
F	ef
G	as in **j'ai**
H	ash
I	ee
J	as in **j'y**
K	Ka
L	el
M	em
N	en
O	oh
P	pay
Q	koo
R	air
S	es
T	tay
U	as in H<u>u</u>gh
V	vay
W	dooble vay
X	ix
Y	ee grek
Z	zed

Useful Phrases

s'il vous plait	please		**Ça va.**	I'm OK.
merci	thank you		**Ça va bien.**	I am well.
Je suis désolé(e)	I am sorry			
Excusez-moi	Excuse me		**Ça va très bien merci.**	
Comment Ça va?	How are you?		I am very well, thank you.	
Ça va?	Are you OK?			
Bof.	So so.		**Ça ne va pas (du tout).**	
			I'm not OK (at all).	

Les salutations/Greetings

bonjour	hello
salut!	hi!
au revoir	goodbye
bonsoir	good evening
bonne nuit	good night
bienvenue	welcome
bon anniversaire	happy birthday
bon voyage	have a good journey
bonne année	happy new year
bonne chance!	good luck!

Le temps/The time

midi	midday
minuit	midnight
heure(s)	o'clock (hours)
et quart	quarter past
et demi(e)	half past
moins le quart	quarter to
Quelle heure est-il?	What time is it?

Il est six heures vingt.
It is twenty past six.

Il est six heures moins vingt.
It is twenty to six.

À quelle heure…? At what time…?

À huit heures et demie.
At half past eight.

Note that **demi** needs an **-e** when it follows an hour, but not when it follows **midi** or **minuit** e.g. **Il est midi et demi.**

 ## Helpful Hint

You also need to be able to understand and use the 24-hour clock.

a.m.
00.10 **Il est zéro heures dix**
01.00 **Il est une heure**
02.15 **Il est deux heures quinze**
05.30 **Il est cinq heures trente**
09.45 **Il est neuf heures quarante-cinq**
p.m.
12.10 **Il est douze heures dix**
13.00 **Il est treize heures**
14.15 **Il est quatorze heures quinze**
17.30 **Il est dix-sept heures trente**
21.45 **Il est vingt et une heures quarante-cinq**

Keywords

une femme	a woman
une fille	a girl
un garçon	a boy
un homme	a man

Les membres de la famille / family members

un mari	a husband
une femme	a wife
un père	a father
une mère	a mother
un beau-père	a father-in-law
une belle-mère	a mother-in-law
papa	dad
maman	mum
un(e) enfant	a child
un fils	a son
une fille	a daughter
un fils / une fille unique	an only child (boy/girl)
un frère	a brother
une sœur	a sister
un demi-frère	a half-brother
une demi-sœur	a half-sister
un beau-frère	a brother-in-law
une belle-sœur	a sister-in-law
un grand-père	grandfather
une grand-mère	grandmother
un oncle	an uncle
une tante	an aunt
un(e) cousin(e)	a cousin
un neveu	a nephew
une nièce	a niece

Les amitiés / friendships

un(e) ami(e)	a friend
un copain	a friend (male)
une copine	a friend (female)
un(e) petit(e) ami(e)	a boy / girlfriend
un(e) voisin(e)	a neighbour
un(e) correspondant(e)	a pen-friend

L'état civil / marital status

célibataire	single
divorcé(e)	divorced
marié(e)	married
séparé(e)	separated
une veuve	a widow
un veuf	a widower

Parler de vous-même / Talking about yourself

Comment t'appelles-tu?	What's your name?
Je m'appelle Michel Borie.	My name is Michel Borie.
Quel âge as-tu?	How old are you?
J'ai vingt-sept ans.	I'm 27 years old.
Quelle est la date de ton anniversaire?	When is your birthday?
C'est le trois mai.	It's the 3rd May.
Où habites-tu?	Where do you live?
J'habite 20 rue de Beauregard à Montluçon.	I live in 20 rue de Beauregard in Montluçon.
Vous êtes marié?	Are you married?
Je suis célibataire.	I am single.
De quelle couleur sont tes yeux?	What colour are your eyes?
J'ai les yeux verts.	I've got green eyes.
Comment sont tes cheveux?	What's your hair like?
J'ai les cheveux bruns et courts.	I've short, brown hair.
Quelle est votre profession?	What is your profession?
Je suis professeur.	I am a teacher.
Comment est ta personnalité?	What's your personality like?
Je suis honnête et intelligent.	I'm honest and intelligent.

 Task

The information on this **Carte d'identité** (identity card) has been mixed up. Can you rearrange it correctly based on the information above?

Carte d'identité

Nom de famille:	Michel
Prénom:	Borie
Age:	le 3 mai
Date de naissance:	20 rue de Beauregard
Situation de famille:	bruns
Adresse:	27 ans
Nationalité:	professeur
Profession:	célibataire
Cheveux:	verts
Yeux:	Français

Family and Friends

Grammaire (Avoir & Etre)

The verbs **avoir** and **être** often get confused. They are very useful, so make sure you know how to use them.

avoir	to have	être	to be
J'ai **un frère.**	I have a brother	Je suis **Anglais**	I'm English
Tu as **un animal?**	Have you a pet?	Tu es **Français?**	Are you French?
Il a **les yeux verts.**	He has green eyes	Il est **sportif**	He is sporty
Elle a **les cheveux longs.**	She has long hair	Elle est **intelligente**	She is clever
Nous avons **un chat.**	We have a cat	Nous sommes **prêts**	We are ready
Vous avez **un stylo?**	Have you a pen?	Vous êtes **marié?**	Are you married?
Ils ont **un lapin.**	They (m) have a rabbit	Ils sont **honnêtes**	They (m) are honest
Elles ont **deux souris.**	They (f) have two mice	Elles sont **des amies**	They (f) are friends

avoir is also used in French for giving ages e.g. J'ai **14 ans** (I have 14 years).

Famille, amis et animaux/Family, friends & pets

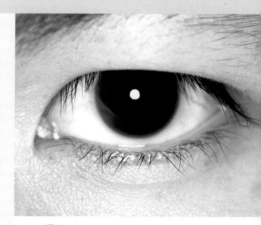

J'ai... I have...	**un frère / une soeur / un copain / une copine, qui s'appelle...** a brother / a sister / a friend (m) / a friend (f), who is called...
J'ai... I have...	**un chat / un cheval / un chien / un cochon d'Inde / un hamster / un lapin / un oiseau / une perruche / un poisson rouge / une souris.** a cat / a horse / a dog / a guinea pig / a hamster / a rabbit / a bird / a budgerigar / a goldfish / a mouse.
Il / Elle est... He / She is...	**grand(e) / petit(e) / de taille moyenne / intelligent(e) / amusant(e) / gentil(le) / généreux (généreuse).** tall / small / medium height / clever / funny / kind / generous.
Il / Elle a... He / She has...	**les cheveux longs / courts / mi-longs / frisés / blonds / bruns / roux / noirs / raides.** long / short / mid-length / curly / blonde / brown / red / black / straight hair.
Et, Il / Elle a... And, he / she has...	**les yeux verts / gris / noisette / bleus.** green / grey / hazel / blue eyes.

🔆 Helpful Hint

Try to extend your answers and make them as interesting as possible.

- Quel âge as-tu?
  J'ai quinze ans, presque 16 ans.
  I'm 15, nearly 16.
  Je viens d'avoir 16 ans.
  I've just turned 16.
  J'aurai 16 ans le deux mai.
  I'll be 16 on the 2nd May.

- As-tu des frères ou des sœurs?
  J'ai un frère qui s'appelle Paul.
  Paul a 13 ans et il aime la télé.
  I've a brother called Paul.
  Paul's 13 and he likes TV.

- Tu as un animal?
  J'ai un chien noir et blanc.
  Il s'appelle Noiraud et il a 3 ans.
  I've a black and white dog.
  He's called Noiraud and he's
  3 years old.

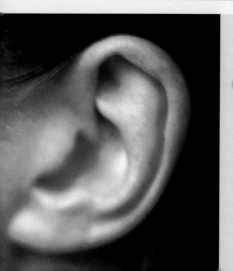

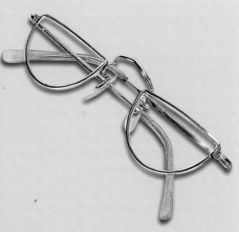

Les métiers/occupations

un agent de police	policeman	**un garçon de café**	waiter
un boucher	butcher	**une hôtesse de l'air**	air hostess
un boulanger	baker	**un infirmier / une infirmière**	nurse
un caissier / une caissière	cashier	**un informaticien**	IT worker
un chauffeur	driver	**un ingénieur**	engineer
un chômeur / une chômeuse	unemployed	**un mécanicien**	a mechanic
un coiffeur / une coiffeuse	hairdresser	**un médecin**	doctor
un dentiste	dentist	**un professeur**	teacher
un directeur / une directrice	head teacher / manager	**un propriétaire**	owner
un(e) employé(e) (de banque)	(bank) employee	**une secrétaire**	secretary
un épicier	grocer	**un serveur / une serveuse**	waiter / waitress
une femme au foyer	housewife	**un vendeur / une vendeuse**	shop assistant
un facteur	postal worker	**un vétérinaire**	vet
un fermier	farmer		

Grammaire (Adjectives)

When using adjectives (describing words), you need to remember two things:

1. In French, most adjectives come after the noun (although some common adjectives like **grand** (big) and **petit** (small) do come before the noun).
2. The ending on the adjective has to match the noun:
   - If the noun is feminine singular add **-e** (unless it ends in **-e** anyway e.g. **rouge**).
   - If the noun is masculine plural add **-s** (unless it ends in **-s** anyway e.g. **gris**).
   - If the noun is feminine plural add **-es**.

un petit chien noir	a small, black dog
une petite perruche bleue	a small, blue budgie
deux chats blancs	two white cats
elle porte des lunettes rondes	she wears round glasses

There are a few special cases that you should know about:
- When a noun is feminine, **blanc** becomes **blanche**.
- Adjectives ending in **-x** change to **-se** when the noun is feminine.
- Adjectives ending in **-f** change to **-ve** when the noun is feminine.

une souris blanche	a white mouse
une tante généreuse	a generous aunt
une fille sportive	a sporty girl

Helpful Hint

When giving someone's occupation there is no need to use **un / une** in front of the noun.

e.g. **Mon père est professeur.**
My father is a teacher.
Ma mère travaille à Paris, elle est dentiste.
My mother works in Paris, she is a dentist.

Test Yourself!

From the descriptions given, identify what each person's occupation might be

e.g. **Il travaille pour la poste.**
Il est facteur.

1. **Il travaille dans un bureau.**
2. **Elle travaille dans une école.**
3. **Il travaille avec des voitures.**
4. **Elle travaille avec les animaux.**

Family and Friends

Elodie, 14 ans

Ma meilleure amie s'appelle Anne-Marie. Elle est très sportive, elle préfère le football et elle joue au tennis. Elle a les yeux bleus et les cheveux longs et frisés. Elle porte des lunettes. Mes parents sont divorcés, mais j'ai deux frères, Thomas et Yves.

Valérie, 16 ans

Je suis fille unique. Mes parents sont très gentils. Ma mère est professeur et mon père est employé de banque. Ma mère a 36 ans, et elle est amusante et généreuse. Mon père a 39 ans et il est intelligent et sportif.

Exam Practice

Thibault, Elodie and Valérie are talking about their families and friends:
1. Who is an only child?
2. Whose parents are divorced?
3. Who has a pet?
4. Who has a sister?
5. Who has two brothers?
6. Whose father works in a bank?
7. Whose friend has long hair?

Thibault, 15 ans

Il y a quatre personnes dans ma famille - mon père, ma mère, ma sœur et moi. Ma sœur s'appelle Chantal et elle a 19 ans. Elle a les cheveux bruns et les yeux verts. Elle est très sympa et intelligente. J'ai un petit lapin blanc qui habite dans le jardin.

Helpful Hint

In the French language, there are three ways of saying *my*, depending on the noun.
- **Mon** is used for *my* with masculine words e.g. mon **père**, mon **lapin**.
- **Ma** is used in front of feminine words e.g. ma **mère**, ma **maison**.
- **Mes** is used with plural words e.g. mes **parents,** mes **frères**.

You also use **mon** in front of words which are feminine, but begin with a vowel e.g. **mon amie, mon école**.

Test Yourself!

In French, how do you say…?
1. my sister-in-law
2. my friends
3. my clever aunt
4. my generous father
5. my big, black cat
6. my small, white mouse

Les sports et loisirs / sports and hobbies

l'alpinisme	mountaineering
l'athlétisme	athletics
le basket	basketball
courir	to run
la course	running
le cyclisme	cycling
la danse	dancing
l'équitation	horse riding
le foot	football
le golf	golf
la gymnastique	gymnastics
le handball	handball
le hockey	hockey
le judo	judo
la natation	swimming
la patin à roulettes	roller skating
patiner	to skate
la pêche	fishing
le ping-pong	table tennis
la planche à voile	windsurfing
la planche à roulettes	skateboarding
les promenades	walks
les randonnées	walks / excursions
le rugby	rugby
le skate	skateboarding
le ski nautique	water-skiing
le tennis	tennis

Les divertissements / entertainment

le bal	a ball (dance)
les boums	parties
le cinéma	cinema
les concerts	concerts
la discothèque	disco / nightclub
les jeux-vidéo	computer games
la musique	music
le théâtre	theatre

Les passe-temps / pastimes

les cartes	cards
les échecs	chess
la lecture	reading
les ordinateurs	computers
la photographie	photography

Grammaire

You will need to know the following verbs to talk about your hobbies, interests and what you do in your free time:

jouer	to play
Je joue **au foot**	I play football
Tu joues **d'un instrument?**	Do you play an instrument?
Il / elle joue **du piano**	He / she plays the piano
Nous jouons **aux cartes**	We play cards
Vous jouez **de la guitare?**	Do you play the guitar?
Ils / Elles jouent **au golf**	They play golf

faire	to do, to make
Je fais **du shopping**	I go shopping
Tu fais **de la voile?**	Do you go sailing?
Il / elle fait **de la natation**	He / she goes swimming
Nous faisons **un gâteau**	We are making a cake
Vous faites **du patinage?**	Do you go skating?
Ils / elles font **du vélo**	They are going cycling

Make sure you know how to use **faire** correctly. It can be confusing because it is often used in French expressions where we would say *to go*.

aller	to go
Je vais **au cinéma**	I'm going to the cinema
Tu vas **à la piscine?**	Are you going to the pool?
Il / elle va **au concert**	He / she is going to the concert
Nous allons **au théâtre**	We are going to the theatre
Vous allez **aux magasins?**	Are you going to the shops?
Ils / elles vont **au stade**	They are going to the stadium

Mes préférences / My preferences

Je préfère...	I prefer...
J'adore...	I love...
J'aime beaucoup...	I like a lot...
Je n'aime pas tellement...	I don't like very much...
Je n'aime pas du tout...	I don't like at all...
Je déteste...	I hate...

J'aime / je n'aime pas..., parce que c'est... I like / I don't like…, because it's…	**amusant / bon pour la santé / passionnant / facile / dangereux / ennuyeux / difficile / barbant.** enjoyable / good for you / exciting / easy / dangerous / boring / difficult / dull.
Je suis membre... I am a member…	**d'un club de natation / d'une équipe de football.** of a swimming club / of a football team.
J'aime lire... I like reading…	**le journal / les magazines / les romans policiers / les bandes dessinées.** the newspaper / magazines / detective novels / comics.
J'aime écouter... I like listening to…	**la musique pop / les disques compacts / la radio.** pop music / CDs / the radio.
Mon acteur / chanteur / auteur / joueur préféré est... , parce qu'il est... My favourite actor / singer / author / player is…, because he is…	**beau / talentueux / amusant / passionnant.** good-looking / talented / funny / exciting.
Mon actrice / ma chanteuse préférée est..., parce qu'elle est... My favourite actress / singer is…, because she is...	**belle / talentueuse / amusante / passionnante.** beautiful / talented / funny / exciting.

 **Helpful Hint**

You can also use the following phrases to help you express your preferences:

Je m'intéresse au foot	I'm interested in football (masculine)
Je m'intéresse à la natation	I'm interested in swimming (feminine)
Je m'intéresse à l'athlétisme	I'm interested in athletics (word begins with vowel)
Je m'intéresse aux échecs	I'm interested in chess (plural)
J'ai horreur du patinage	I can't stand skating (masculine)
J'ai horreur de la lecture	I can't stand reading (feminine)
J'ai horreur de l'équitation	I can't stand horse-riding (word begins with vowel)
J'ai horreur des films d'amour	I can't stand romantic films (plural)

Make sure you use the correct determiner (highlighted), depending on whether the subject is masculine, feminine, singular or plural.

 **Test Yourself!**

In French, how do you say…?
1. I play hockey
2. I go running
3. I do judo
4. I do gymnastics
5. I go to concerts
6. He plays chess
7. She goes to the cinema
8. We go to the shops
9. We play cards
10. I go sailing

Combien de fois?/ How often?

régulièrement	regularly
souvent	often
chaque jour	every day
une fois par semaine	once a week
deux fois par mois	twice a month
de temps en temps	from time to time/ occasionally

? Test Yourself!

Answer these questions in full, saying how frequently you do each activity.

1. Tu vas souvent à la piscine?
2. Tu vas souvent au cinéma?
3. Vous faites souvent du shopping?
4. Vous jouez souvent au foot?
5. Tu joues souvent aux cartes?

Task

1. Match each activity below with the appropriate venue:
   - la natation, l'athlétisme, le foot, la pêche, le patinage sur glace
   - la patinoire, le stade, le terrain de sports, la piscine, le lac
2. Complete the following phrases and give a reason for each answer.
   - Mon sport préféré est...
   - Comme loisirs, j'aime...
   - Dans mon temps libre, je n'aime pas...

Exam Practice

A wide vocabulary and a knowledge of how different words relate to each other is essential if you want to do your best in reading and listening tests. For example, you need to know that **la natation** means swimming, but **nager** means to swim and **la piscine** means swimming pool but **un maillot de bain** means swimming costume. Read the statements below:

A. Le week-end, j'aime aller à la <u>piscine</u>, où je fais de la <u>natation</u> avec mes amies. J'adore <u>nager</u>, c'est bon pour la santé.

B. Le week-end, j'aime faire de l'équitation. J'aime me promener à cheval à la campagne.

C. Le week-end, je fais souvent du cyclisme. Je fais du vélo avec mon ami, Robert. Pour mon anniversaire, je vais recevoir une nouvelle bicyclette.

D. J'adore la lecture. Je préfère les livres de science-fiction, mais j'aime aussi lire des bandes dessinées et des romans d'aventures. Le samedi, je vais à la bibliothèque.

1. Who likes cycling?
2. Who enjoys swimming?
3. Who reads a lot?
4. Who likes horse-riding?
5. In each statement, underline all the words that relate to that particular hobby. The first one has been done for you.

erests and Hobbies

Une Invitation / An Invitation

👤 **Je vais jouer au baseball avec mes amis demain. Tu veux venir avec moi?**
I am going to play baseball with my friends tomorrow. Do you want to come with me?

👤 **Oui, je veux bien. Ce sera amusant.**
Yes please, that would be fun.

👤 **On joue au parc. Tu veux me rencontrer à l'arrêt d'autobus demain matin?**
We play in the park. Do you want to meet me at the bus stop tomorrow morning?

👤 **D'accord. A quelle heure?**
OK. What time?

👤 **A dix heures. Ça va?**
10am. Is that OK?

👤 **Super. A demain.**
Great. See you tomorrow.

💡 Helpful Hint

It is important to make your responses as interesting as possible. Try to include information about when, where, why, how, who with etc.

Le samedi, j'aime aller au cinéma à Manchester avec mon amie, Sarah, pour voir des films comiques. Nous y allons par le train. Mon acteur préféré est Harry Sourire.
On Saturdays, I like going to the cinema in Manchester with my friend Sarah, to see comedy films. We go there by train. My favourite actor is Harry Sourire.

✏️ Task

1️⃣ Complete the following sentences by inserting the correct past participles into the gaps:
   - **J'ai .... mon walkman.**
   - **J'ai .... la télé.**
   - **J'ai .... à la discothèque.**
   - **J'ai .... à la piscine.**
   - **J'ai .... au foot.**
   - **Je suis .... au cinéma.**

2️⃣ Write a description of what you did last weekend. Try to include as much detail as possible.
   Le week-end dernier...

Grammaire (Perfect Tense)

In normal conversation you often talk about things that you did in the past, whether it be last night or last year, so you need to be able to do the same in French.

To form the perfect tense, which is used to talk about actions and events that have been completed, you use **avoir** (to have) in the correct form, followed by the past participle of the verb. For most verbs, this means using the ending **-é**.

J'ai joué	I played	**J'ai écouté**	I listened to
J'ai regardé	I watched	**J'ai nagé**	I swam
J'ai dansé	I danced	**J'ai chanté**	I sang

Note that **Je suis allé** is *I went* for a male and **Je suis allée** is *I went* for a female. There are some irregular past participles e.g. **J'ai lu** (I read) and **J'ai fait** (I made / did).

Les domiciles/homes/residences

chez	at the house of...
chez moi	at my house
chez mon ami	at my friend's house
Mon adresse est...	My address is...
Le code postal est...	The post code is...

Les salles/rooms

une cave	cellar
une chambre	bedroom
une cuisine	kitchen
un salon	lounge
les WC	toilet
une salle à manger /de bains /de séjour	
dining room / bathroom / living room	

Les meubles/furniture

une armoire	wardrobe
un canapé	sofa
une chaîne-stéréo	hi-fi
une chaise	chair
le chauffage central	central heating
une cuisinière	cooker
une douche	shower
un escalier	stairs
un fauteuil	armchair
une fenêtre	window
un four à micro-ondes	microwave oven
un frigo	fridge
un lavabo	sink
un lave-vaisselle	dishwasher
un lit	bed
une machine à laver	washing machine
un miroir	mirror
une moquette	fitted carpet
un mur	wall
un placard	cupboard
une porte	door
un réveil	alarm clock
un rideau	curtain
un tapis	carpet
un téléphone	telephone

Le jardin/garden

un arbre	tree
une fleur	flower
le gazon	grass
la pelouse	lawn

Où habitez-vous?/Where do you live?

J'habite ... I live...	dans une maison /dans un appartement / une ferme /dans un pavillon. in a house/in a flat/on a farm/in a bungalow.
C'est dans... It is in...	un village /le centre de ville /la banlieue / la campagne /un immeuble. a village/the town centre/the suburbs/ the countryside/a block of flats.
J'aime habiter ici parce que... I like living here because...	j'ai ma propre chambre /c'est très tranquille / c'est pratique /c'est pittoresque /c'est près des magasins /c'est animé / le jardin est joli / la vue est spectaculaire. I have my own room/it's very quiet/it's practical/ it's picturesque/it's near the shops/it's lively/ the garden is pretty/the view is spectacular.
Je n'aime pas habiter ici parce que... I don't like living here because...	je partage une chambre avec mon frère / c'est trop calme /c'est bruyant /c'est loin des magasins /c'est moche /ma chambre est trop petite /il n'y a rien à faire /c'est pollué. I share a room with my brother/it's too quiet/it's noisy/it's a long way from the shops/it's ugly/my room is too small/there's nothing to do/it is polluted.

 Helpful Hint

When describing your house, you will find the phrase **il y a** very useful. It means both *there is* and *there are*.

e.g.
- **Ma maison est grande. Il y a 7 pièces.** — My house is large. There are seven rooms.
- **Il y a deux jardins, devant et derrière la maison.** — There are two gardens, in front and behind the house.
- **Au-rez-de-chaussée, il y a un salon.** — Downstairs, there is a living room.
- **Au premier étage, il y a trois chambres.** — Upstairs, there are three bedrooms.
- **Dans ma chambre, il y a une armoire.** — In my room, there is a wardrobe.

If you want to say that *there is not* something, you need to say **il n'y a pas**.

e.g.
- **Il y a une machine à laver, mais il n'y a pas de lave-vaisselle.** — There is a washing machine, but there isn't a dishwasher.
- **Il y a une table, mais il n'y a pas d'armoire.** — There is a table, but there's no wardrobe.

Notice that when you use a negative, the **un** or **une** changes to **de** (**d'** before a vowel).

Local Environment

Grammaire (Prepositions)

Prepositions normally come before a noun. The following examples can all be used to describe where something is in relation to something else:

Dans ma maison, il y a quatre chambres.	*In* my house, there are 4 bedrooms.
Devant la maison, il y a un jardin.	*In front of* the house, there's a garden.
La chaise est sur la table.	The chair is *on* the table.
Le chat est sous le lit.	The cat is *under* the bed.
Le jardin est derrière la maison.	The garden is *behind* the house.
La cuisine est entre le salon et les WC.	The kitchen is *between* the lounge and the toilet.

Notice the difference between the masculine and feminine for the following phrases:

à côté de	next to	**en face de**	opposite
à gauche de	to the left of	**à droite de**	to the right of

La cuisine est à côté du salon.	The kitchen is next *to* the lounge (m)
Mon lit est à côté de la table.	My bed is next *to* the table (f)

? Test Yourself!

In French, how do you say…?
1. There is a table in the living room.
2. The telephone is on the table.
3. There isn't a microwave in the kitchen.
4. The wardrobe is between the bed and the door.
5. It's under the window.

Task

Read the following description and see if you can draw a plan of the bedroom using the information you are given.

Dans ma chambre, à gauche, il y a un lit. A droite, il y a une armoire. Entre le lit et l'armoire, il y a une petite table. Sur la table, il y a une lampe. A côté de la lampe, il y a une plante. Sous le lit, il y a un chat. Devant l'armoire, il y a une chaise.

Exam Practice

Sabine and Jean-Pierre are talking about where they live. Make a list of all the differences between their houses.

Sabine: **J'habite dans la banlieue de Lyon. Ma maison est assez grande et moderne. Au rez-de-chaussée, il y a une salle de séjour, une salle à manger et une petite cuisine. Au premier étage, il y a trois chambres et une salle de bains. J'ai ma propre chambre. Le garage est à côté de la maison. Nous avons un grand jardin derrière la maison. J'aime habiter ici parce que c'est tranquille.**

Jean-Pierre: **J'habite dans le centre de Lyon. Ma maison est assez petite et moderne. Au rez-de-chaussée, il y a une salle de séjour et une grande cuisine. Au premier étage, il y a deux chambres et une salle de bains. Je partage ma chambre avec mon frère, Alain. Le garage est à côté de la maison. Nous avons un grand jardin devant la maison. Je n'aime pas habiter ici parce que c'est bruyant.**

Home and

Localité/Location

Ma ville se trouve dans... My town is located in...	**le nord/l'ouest/l'est/le sud/le nord-ouest/ le centre de l'Angleterre.** the north/the west/the east/the south/the north-west/ the centre of England.
C'est située... It is situated...	**au bord de la mer/à côté de la rivière/ dans les montagnes.** by the sea/beside a river/in the mountains.
C'est... It is...	**une ville industrielle/touristique/historique.** an industrial/tourist/historic town.
Il y a... There are...	**cent cinquante mille/seulement cinq cents habitants.** 150,000/just 500 inhabitants.
Au centre -ville, il y a... In the town centre, there is/are...	**beaucoup de monuments intéressants/quelques distractions/un centre commercial/un hôtel de ville/un musée/une église/une cathédrale/ un château/une mairie/une plage/un port / des bâtiments historiques.** lots of interesting monuments/a few attractions/ a shopping centre/a town hall/a museum/a church/ a cathedral/a castle/a town hall (small town)/a beach/ a port/some historical buildings.
L'endroit... The area...	**est très agréable/n'est pas très joli/ est pittoresque/est moche.** is very pleasant/is not very nice/is picturesque/is unattractive.
Il y a... There is/are...	**beaucoup d'espaces verts/les champs/la forêt/ trop d'usines/les routes trafic bruyantes.** lots of green spaces/fields/the forest/too many factories/noisy roads.

(?) Test Yourself!

In French, how do you say...?
1. France is bigger than England.
2. Rouen is smaller than Paris.
3. There are less parks but more historic buildings.
4. The south of England is hotter than the north.

Helpful Hint

You need to be able to compare different towns and places. To do this, you will find **plus** (more) and **moins** (less) invaluable.

Il y a plus...	There are more...	**Il y a moins...**	There are less...
plus chaud	hotter (more hot)	**moins chaud**	colder (less hot)
plus grand	bigger (more big)	**moins grand**	smaller (less big)

e.g. **Londres est plus grand que Manchester.**
London is bigger than Manchester.
Dans la ville il y a plus de magasins que dans le village.
In town there are more shops than in the village.

Local Environment

Grammaire (Adjectives)

In French, most adjectives come after the noun they describe (see page 8). However, the following useful adjectives all come before the noun:

grand large   **petit** small   **nouveau** new
vieux old   **joli** pretty   **beau** beautiful

e.g. **J'habite une** grande **ville industrielle.** I live in a large, industrial town.
     J'habite un joli **village pittoresque.** I live in a pretty, picturesque village.

Notice the feminine and plural forms of **beau**, **vieux** and **nouveau**:

beau (m)   **belle** (f)   **beaux** (m/p)   **belles** (f/p)
vieux (m)   **vieille** (f)   **vieux** (m/p)   **vieilles** (f/p)
nouveau (m)   **nouvelle** (f)   **nouveaux** (m/p)   **nouvelles** (f/p)

These three adjectives also have a special masculine form, which is used before nouns that start with a vowel or silent **h**:

e.g. **un** bel **homme**   a good-looking man
     un vieil **appartement**   an old flat
     le nouvel **an**   the new year

 ? Test Yourself!

How do you say…?
1. a new flat
2. an old house
3. a new armchair
4. old carpets
5. beautiful, new curtains

Chantal: J'habite dans une grande ville industrielle qui s'appelle Lille. C'est dans le nord de la France. J'aime bien ma ville parce que c'est très animé. Il y a beaucoup de choses à faire. Le désavantage d'habiter ici, c'est que l'air est assez pollué.

Patricia: J'habite à Valras, une ville touristique au bord de la mer dans le sud de la France. C'est une belle ville avec beaucoup de touristes. On peut visiter la plage, le casino et le musée. Les restaurants sont très bons. J'adore habiter ici!

Exam Practice

1. Who lives by the sea?
2. Why does Chantal like living where she does?
3. How does Patricia feel about the place where she lives?
4. Name one disadvantage given for living in an industrial town.
5. Name one advantage given for living in a tourist town.

 Helpful Hint

In addition to **Il y a** (there is / there are), you will find **on peut** (you can / one can) very useful when talking about where you live.
e.g. **Il y a une piscine. On peut faire de la natation.** There's a pool. You can go swimming.

Task

Sort the following phrases into pairs.
e.g. **Il y a un stade. On peut regarder des matches de foot.**

1. **Il y a un cinéma.**
2. **Il y a un centre commercial.**
3. **Il y a une gare.**
4. **Il y a un aéroport.**
5. **Il y a un musée.**
6. **Il y a une bibliothèque.**
A. **On peut visiter des expositions.**
B. **On peut faire du shopping.**
C. **On peut emprunter des livres.**
D. **On peut regarder des films.**
E. **On peut prendre le train.**
F. **On peut prendre l'avion.**

La routine quotidienne/daily routine

Tu te lèves à quelle heure? Qu'est-ce que tu fais le matin?
What time do you get up? What do you do in the morning?
Je me lève à sept heures. Je me lave, me brosse les dents, me brosse les cheveux et je mets mon uniforme scolaire.
I get up at 7 o'clock. I have a wash, brush my teeth, brush my hair and I put on my school uniform.

Comment vas-tu au collège? Tu rentres à quelle heure?
How do you get to school? What time do you get home?
Je vais au collège à pied. Je rentre vers quatre heures moins le quart.
I go to school on foot. I get home about quarter to 4.

Tu prends le petit-déjeuner à quelle heure? Tu quittes la maison à quelle heure?
What time do you have breakfast? What time do you leave the house?
Je ne prends pas de petit-déjeuner. Je quitte la maison vers huit heures et quart.
I don't have any breakfast. I leave at about quarter past 8.

Qu'est-ce que tu fais le soir? Tu te couches à quelle heure?
What do you do in the evening? What time do you go to bed?
Je change mes vêtements. Puis, je prends le dîner, je fais mes devoirs et je regarde la télé ou je sors. Je me couche vers dix heures et demie.
I change my clothes. Then I have dinner, do my homework and watch TV or I go out. I go to bed at about 10.30.

Grammaire (Reflexive Verbs)

To talk about your daily routine, you will often need to use *reflexive* verbs. A reflexive verb describes an action that you do *to* or *for* yourself. They require a *special pronoun* before the verb:

e.g. **Je lave (la voiture)**	I wash (the car).
Je me lave	I wash myself
Tu réveilles (ton père)	You wake (your father)
Tu te réveilles	You wake up
Il brosse (le chien)	He is brushing (the dog)
Il se brosse (les dents)	He is brushing (his teeth)

The pronouns **me**, **te** and **se** change to **m'**, **t'** and **s'** before a vowel or a silent 'h'
e.g. **Je m'appelle, je m'habille, elle s'appelle, elle s'habille**.
Here are two reflexive verbs in full:

se laver	to wash oneself	**s'habiller**	to get dressed
je me lave	I wash myself	**je m'habille**	I get dressed
tu te laves	you wash yourself	**tu t'habilles**	you get dressed
il se lave	he washes himself	**il s'habille**	he gets dressed
elle se lave	she washes herself	**elle s'habille**	she gets dressed
nous nous lavons	we wash ourselves	**nous nous habillons**	we get dressed
vous vous lavez	you wash yourself	**vous vous habillez**	you get dressed
ils/elles se lavent	they wash themselves	**ils/elles s'habillent**	they get dressed

Daily Routine

Helpful Hint

When you are describing your daily routine, you can make it more interesting by using adverbs of time.

D'habitude, **je me lève à sept heures du matin.** — *Usually*, I get up at 7.30am.
Puis, **je me douche dans la salle de bains.** — *Then*, I shower in the bathroom.
Ensuite, **je prends le petit-déjeuner.** — *Afterwards*, I have breakfast.
Avant **de quitter la maison, je me lave.** — *Before* leaving the house, I wash.
Le soir, **je rentre à la maison.** — *In the evening*, I come home.
D'abord, **je fais mes devoirs.** — *First of all*, I do my homework.
Après, **je regarde la télé.** — *After that* I watch TV.
Enfin, **je me couche à dix heures du soir.** — *Finally*, I go to bed at 10pm.
En semaine, **je me lève de bonne heure.** — *During the week*, I get up early.
Le week-end, **je me lève plus tard.** — *At the weekend*, I get up later.

You can make your descriptions more sophisticated by linking phrases together to form longer sentences, for example...

D'habitude, je me lève vers sept heures, puis je me lave dans la salle de bains et avant de prendre le petit-déjeuner, je m'habille dans ma chambre.
Usually, I get up around 7 o'clock, then I have a wash in the bathroom and, before having breakfast, I get dressed in my bedroom.

Useful Phrases

- **se baigner**	to bathe
- **je me baigne**	I bathe
- **se brosser les dents**	to brush one's teeth
- **je me brosse les dents**	I brush my teeth
- **se dépêcher**	to hurry
- **je me dépêche**	I hurry
- **se doucher**	to shower
- **je me douche**	I shower
- **se peigner**	to comb
- **je me peigne**	I comb
- **se raser**	to shave
- **je me rase**	I shave
- **aller au lit**	to go to bed
- **je vais au lit**	I go to bed
- **faire les devoirs**	to do one's homework
- **je fais mes devoirs**	I do my homework
- **prendre un bain**	to take a bath
- **je prends un bain**	I take a bath

Test Yourself!

In French, how do you say...?
1 During the week, I go to bed early.
2 At the weekend, I go to bed later.
3 Usually, I go to school by bus.
4 First of all, I have a shower and shave.
5 In the evening, I have a bath and watch television.

Task

Write a description of your own daily routine using the phrases below to get you started.
En semaine, je me lève à...
Je prends le petit-déjeuner dans...
Je vais au collège en...
Le soir, je fais mes devoirs, puis je...
Enfin, je me couche vers...

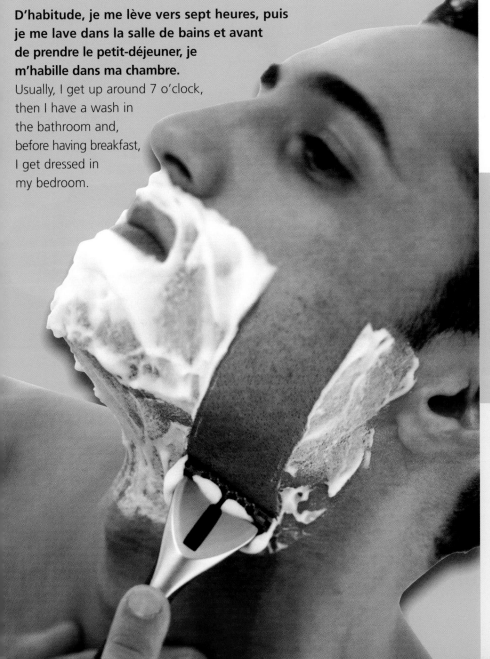

Les repas / meals

le petit-déjeuner	breakfast
le déjeuner	lunch
le goûter	afternoon tea
le dîner	evening meal

Nourriture et boisson / food and drink*

les bonbons	sweets
le café	coffee
le café-crème	white coffee (with cream)
les céréales	breakfast cereals
les chips	crisps
le chocolat-chaud	hot chocolate
le croissant	French pastry
l'eau	water
les frites	chips
le fruit	fruit
le gâteau	cake
le jus d'orange	orange juice
le lait	milk
le pain	bread
le pain grillé	toast
le potage	soup
le sandwich	sandwich
le thé	tea
la viande	meat
la viande rotie	roast meat
le yaourt	yoghurt

*A comprehensive list of food and drink can be found on page 39.

Useful Phrases

Je suis végétarien. Je ne mange pas de viande.
I am vegetarian. I do not eat meat.
Je mange dans la canteen du collège.
I eat in the school canteen.
J'aime la cantine. Il y a toujours un bon choix de plats.
I like the canteen. There is always a good choice of dishes.
Je déteste la cantine. La cuisine y est dégoûtante.
I hate the canteen. The food there is disgusting.
D'habitude, pour le déjeuner je mange / je bois…
Usually, for lunch I eat / I drink…
J'apporte des sandwiches au collège.
I take sandwiches to school.
À la récréation, je mange des chips ou des fruits.
At break time, I eat crisps or fruit.

(?) Test Yourself!

In French, how do you say…?
1. For breakfast, I eat toast and cereal.
2. For lunch, I like to eat soup or a sandwich in the school canteen.
3. Usually, for tea I eat cake and drink hot chocolate.
4. I like to drink tea. I don't like coffee.
5. In the evening, for dinner, I eat meat and vegetables or fish and chips.

Daily Routine

Exam Practice

Monique and Patrick are talking about their daily routines:
1. Who drinks orange juice for breakfast?
2. Who has a pet?
3. Who likes jogging?
4. Who gets up earlier?
5. Who goes to bed later?
6. Who has a rather unhealthy lifestyle?

Patrick: **Je me réveille à huit heures, mais je reste au lit et je me lève à huit heures et demie. Pour le petit-déjeuner, je prends du chocolat chaud, des croissants, du pain, de la confiture et des petits gâteaux. Je vais au travail en voiture. Le soir, je mange des frites. Je regarde la télé. J'aime manger des chocolats en regardant la télévision. Je me couche à minuit.**

Monique: **D'habitude, je me lève de bonne heure. Avant le petit-déjeuner, je fais du jogging. Pour le petit-déjeuner, je prends un jus d'orange et des céréales. Après, je me douche et je m'habille. Je vais au travail à vélo. Le soir, je vais au gymnase avant de rentrer. Pour le dîner, je mange une salade. Je promène le chien et je me couche à neuf heures et demie.**

L'argent de poche / pocket money

Je reçois de l'argent de poche.
I get pocket money.

Je dois travailler pour gagner mon argent de poche.
I have to work to earn pocket money.

Mes parents sont généreux / ce n'est pas assez!
My parents are generous / it isn't enough!

Je dois acheter mes propres vêtements.
I have to buy my own clothes.

J'ai besoin d'argent pour aller en vacances.
I need money to go on holiday.

Avec l'argent, j'achète...
With the money, I buy...

Je fais des économies.
I'm saving money.

Task

1. In French, write an account of your eating habits on a typical school day. Provide as much information as possible e.g. what, when, where, who with and your opinions.

2. Practise saying the following, filling in the gaps to complete the phrases:
   - **Mes parents me donnent... livres par semaine.**
     My parents give me... pounds a week.
   - **Avec mon argent de poche, j'achète...**
     With my pocket money, I buy...
   - **J'économise... livres par mois.**
     I save... pounds a month.

Keywords

un cours	a lesson	un règlement	a rule
un échange	an exchange	un sondage	a survey
un / une élève	a pupil	un stylo	a pen
un emploi du temps	a timetable	un tableau (noir)	a blackboard
une épreuve	a test	un atelier	a workshop
les études	studies	un centre sportif	a sports centre
un examen	an exam	une cour	a playground
la pause-déjeuner	lunch break	un laboratoire	a lab
la récréation	break time	une salle de classe	a classroom
un trimestre	a term	décrire	to describe
les grandes vacances	summer holidays	dessiner	to draw
l'appel (m)	the register	écrire	to write
un bic	a ball point pen	épeler	to spell
un cahier	an exercise book	étudier	to study
un crayon	a pencil	dire	to say
une gomme	a rubber	faire attention	to pay attention
un livre	a book	passer	to sit (an exam)
le papier	paper	poser	to ask (questions)
une règle	a ruler		

Mon collège / my school

Fais une description de ton école. Comment s'appelle ton collège? Combien d'élèves y a-t-il?
Describe your school. What's your school called? How many pupils are there?

Mon collège s'appelle Sainte Isabelle. Il y a mille cinq cents élèves. Mon collège n'est pas grand. Les bâtiments sont assez modernes. Il y a une bibliothèque et un gymnase, mais il n'y a pas de piscine.
My school is called St. Isabelle's. There are 1500 pupils. My school isn't big. The buildings are quite modern. There is a library and a gym, but there isn't a pool.

Comment est ton uniforme?
What is your uniform like?

A mon avis, l'uniforme est moche. Je porte un pantalon noir, une chemise blanche et une cravate bleue. Les filles portent une jupe noire.
In my opinion, the uniform is ugly. I wear black trousers, a white shirt and a blue tie. The girls wear a black skirt.

A quelle heure commencent les cours? Quelle est ta matière préférée et pourquoi?
What time do lessons start? What is your favourite subject and why?

Les cours commencent à neuf heures. Je préfère l'histoire parce que c'est intéressant.
Lessons start at 9 o'clock. I prefer history because it's interesting.

Helpful Hint

To add a bit of variety when you are talking about the different subjects, try to use the pronouns **le**, **la** and **les**:

Use **le** for masculine subjects (**français, anglais, dessin etc.**)
Use **la** for feminine subjects (**géographie, physique, histoire etc.**)
Use **les** for plural subjects (**sciences, maths, travaux manuels**)

J'adore le dessin parce que je le trouve amusant.
I love art because I think it's (I find it) fun.

Je déteste la géographie parce que je la trouve ennuyeuse.
I hate geography because I find it boring.
(NB feminine ending on adjective)

Je n'aime pas les sciences parce que je les trouve difficiles.
I don't like science because I find it difficult.
(NB plural ending on adjective)

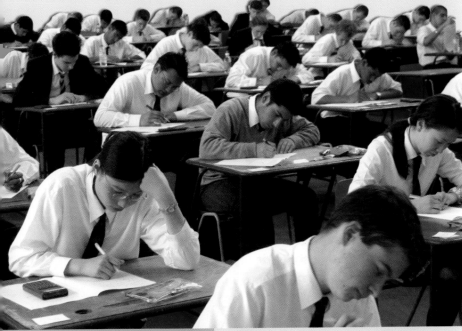

Les matières / The subjects

l'allemand (m)	German
l'anglais (m)	English
l'art dramatique (m)	drama
la biologie	biology
la chimie	chemistry
le dessin	art
l'éducation physique	PE
l'espagnol	Spanish
le français	French
la géographie	geography
l'histoire (f)	history
l'informatique (m)	ICT
l'instruction civique	citizenship
les maths	maths
la musique	music
la physique	physics
la religion	RE
la technologie	technology
les sciences	science
les travaux manuels	craft subjects

Les opinions positives / Positive opinions

J'adore le dessin parce que c'est amusant.
I love art because it's fun.

c'est super	it's great
c'est intéressant	it's interesting
c'est facile	it's easy
c'est amusant	it's funny
c'est génial	it's very good
le prof est sympa	the teacher is nice

Tu es en quelle classe? / Which class are you in?

Je suis en seconde.
I'm in Year 11.

En France	En Grande-Bretagne
sixième	Year 7
cinquième	Year 8
quatrième	Year 9
troisième	Year 10
seconde	Year 11
première	Year 12
terminale	Year 13

? Test Yourself!

1. **Comment s'appelle ton collège?**
2. **Fais une description de ton école.**
3. **Comment est ton uniforme?**
4. Talk about the subjects you study at school by completing the following phrases: **Je fais...**
   Ma matière préférée, c'est...
   Je déteste...
5. Say what you think of the following subjects (e.g. **l'anglais, je le trouve nul**):
   Le français...
   Les maths...
   La technologie...

Les opinions negatives / Negative opinions

Je déteste la géographie parce que c'est ennuyeuse.
I hate geography because it's boring.

c'est nul	it's rubbish
c'est ennuyeux	it's boring
c'est difficile	it's difficult
c'est barbant	it's dull
c'est affreux	it's terrible
le prof est sévère	the teacher is strict

Grammaire (Future Plans)

To talk about your future plans, use **aller** (to go) + the infinitive of the verb
e.g. **Je vais étudier les maths** I'm going to study maths.

Here is the verb **aller** in full:

Je vais **passer le bac.**	I'm going to do A levels.
Tu vas **quitter l'école?**	Are you going to leave school?
Il va **trouver du travail.**	He's going to find a job.
Elle va **devenir mécanicienne.**	She's going to become a mechanic.
Nous allons **aller à l'université.**	We're going to go to university.
Vous allez **faire un stage?**	Are you going to do a course?
Ils vont **apprendre à conduire.**	They're going to learn to drive.
Elles vont **gagner de l'argent.**	They're going to earn some money.

Useful Phrases

Après mes examens, je vais…
After my exams, I am going to…

A l'avenir, je veux …
In the future, I want to…

Pendant les grandes vacances, j'espère…
During the summer holidays, I hope to…

En été, je voudrais…
In the summer, I would like to…

continuer mes études
continue my studies

être dentiste
be a dentist

travailler dans un restaurant
work in a restaurant

trouver un petit emploi
find a part-time job

prendre une année sabbatique
take a year out (a gap year)

faire le tour du monde
travel around the world

rester chez mon correspondant
stay with my pen-friend

Exam Practice

Elodie and Jean-Yves are talking about their plans for the future:

1. Who would like to go to university?
2. Who wants to study ICT?
3. Who wants to become a mechanic?
4. Who would like to travel?
5. Who wants to buy a car?

Jean-Yves: **Je vais quitter l'école en juillet. Je voudrais trouver du travail. J'espère devenir mécanicien. Je veux gagner de l'argent parce que je voudrais acheter une voiture.**

Elodie: **Je vais continuer mes études et j'espère passer le bac. Je voudrais aller à l'université et je veux étudier l'informatique et l'allemand. Je vais aussi visiter l'Australie.**

 Task

Provide information about your **journée scolaire** (school day) by completing the following useful phrases.

- **Les cours commencent à...**
  Lessons start at...
- **Les cours finissent à...**
  Lessons finish at...
- **Nous avons ... cours par jour.**
  We have ... lessons each day.
- **Chaque cours dure...**
  Each lesson lasts...
- **Nous avons la récréation à...**
  We have break at...
- **Le déjeuner est à...**
  Lunch is at...
- **Nous avons ... heure(s) de devoirs par jour.**
  We have... hour(s) of homework every day.

Dans la salle de classe / In the classroom

Levez-vous!	Stand up!
Asseyez-vous!	Sit down!
Taisez-vous!	Be quiet!
Ouvrez vos cahiers.	Open you exercise books.
Je comprends.	I understand.
Je ne comprends pas.	I don't understand.
Comment ça s'écrit?	How is that spelled?
Comment dit-on... en français?	How do you say... in French?
Que veut dire... en anglais?	How do you say...in English?
Qu'est-ce que ça veut dire?	What does that mean?
Tu peux me prêter...?	Can you lend me...?
Tu veux m'aider?	Can you help me?
Je n'ai pas de...	I don't have…
Je ne sais pas.	I don't know.
Je peux avoir...?	Can I have…?
De rien.	Don't mention it (no problem).

D'autres activités / other activities

Je fais partie de l'équipe de football.	I am part of the football team.
Je suis membre du club d'échecs.	I am a member of a chess club.
Je joue dans l'orchestre de l'école.	I play in the school orchestra.
Nous nous entraînons le mardi et le jeudi soir.	We practise on Tuesday and Thursday evenings.
Nous nous rencontrons le mercredi à la pause-déjeuner.	We meet on Wednesday lunch times.

? **Test Yourself!**

1 In French, how would you say...?
- I'm going to go to university.
- He's going to leave school.
- We're going to do A-levels.
- Can you lend me a pen?
- Please can I have some paper?
- I don't have a book.
- I don't understand. What does that mean?

2 Translate the following sentences into English:
- **Je veux trouver du travail.**
- **J'espère aller à l'université.**
- **Je voudrais devenir professeur.**

Travel, Transport

Keywords

un avion	aeroplane	**une carte**	map
un autobus	bus	**un arrêt d'autobus**	bus stop
un car	coach	**une gare**	railway station
une moto	motorbike	**une gare routière**	bus station
un train	train	**un parking**	car park
un vélo	bicycle	**une station**	underground station
une voiture / auto	car	**une station-service**	service station
un piéton	pedestrian	**un aéroport**	airport
un automobiliste	motorist	**un vol**	a flight

Useful Phrases

Pardon, madame!
Excuse me, madam!
Pour aller au port?
How do I get to the port?

Excusez-moi, monsieur! Pour aller à Cannes?
Excuse me, sir! How do I get to Cannes?
**Quittez l'autoroute à la prochaine sortie
et continuez tout droit au rond-pont.**
Leave the motorway at the next exit and
continue straight ahead at the roundabout.

Pour aller à la plage?
How do I get to the beach?
**Prenez la deuxième rue à droite.
Traversez le pont et tournez à
gauche aux feux.**
Take the second road on the right. Cross
the bridge and turn left at the lights.

Où est l'office du tourisme, s'il vous plaît?
Where is the tourist office, please?
**Tournez à gauche, continuez jusqu'au carrefour
et c'est en face de la gare sur la droite.**
Turn left, carry on as far as the crossroads and it's
opposite the station on the right.

Il y a une banque près d'ici?
Is there a bank nearby?
**Tournez à droite, traversez la place
et prenez la première rue à gauche.**
Turn right, cross the square and take
the first road on the left.

d Finding the Way

(?) Test Yourself!

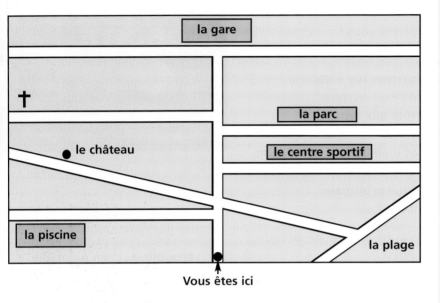

Vous êtes ici

Using the plan, link up the questions with the correct responses.

e.g. Où est le château, s'il vous plaît? C'est la deuxième rue à gauche.

Pour aller à la plage? Continuez tout droit.
Il y a une piscine près d'ici? C'est la première rue à gauche.
Pour aller au parc, s'il vous plaît? C'est la première rue à droite.
Où est la cathédrale, s'il vous plaît? C'est la deuxième rue à droite.
Pour aller à la gare? C'est la troisième rue à gauche.
Il y a un centre sportif près d'ici? C'est la troisième rue à droite.

On achète des billets / Buying tickets

👤 **Je voudrais un aller-simple / aller retour pour Paris.**
I'd like a single / return ticket for Paris.

👤 **Quelle classe voulez-vous?**
What class would you like?

👤 **Première / deuxième classe, s'il vous plaît.**
First class / second class, please.

👤 **Une place fumeur ou non-fumeur?**
A smoking or no-smoking seat?

👤 **Non-fumeur. À quelle heure part le prochain train pour Paris?**
No-smoking. What time is the next train for Paris?

👤 **Le prochain train part à quatorze heures trente.**
The next train leaves at 14:30.

👤 **Le train part de quel quai?**
What platform does it leave from?

👤 **Quai numéro 6, monsieur.**
Platform 6, sir.

👤 **Merci beaucoup. Donnez-moi un horaire, s'il vous plaît.**
Thank you very much. Can I have a timetable, please?

A la gare / At the station

l'entrée	entrance / way in
la sortie	exit / way out
la sortie de secours	emergency exit
police-secours	police assistance
arrivée	arrival
départs	departure
les renseignements	information
un horaire	timetable
le guichet	ticket office
un billet	a ticket
un carnet	a book of tickets
composter	validate ticket
une valise	suitcase
les bagages	luggage
la consigne (automatique)	left luggage (lockers)
la salle d'attente	waiting room
défense de fumer	no smoking
quai	platform
ligne	line

Dans la voiture / In the car

le péage	toll booth
le gazole	diesel fuel
l'essence	petrol
l'essence sans plomb	unleaded petrol
un feu rouge	a red light
défense de stationner	no parking
les freins	brakes
le moteur	engine
la roue	wheel
tomber en panne	to break down
le permis (de conduire)	(driving) licence
une autoroute (e.g. la A6)	motorway
la Route Nationale (e.g. la N7)	a national road
ma voiture ne marche pas	my car won't go

Travel, Transport

Grammaire (The Imperative)

Imperatives are commands - they tell people what to do.

To give directions, instructions or orders, start with the **vous** form of the verb in the present tense. Remove the **vous** and you are left with a command.

prendre	vous prenez	**Prenez la deuxième rue à gauche.**
to take	you take	Take the second road on the left.
tourner	vous tournez	**Tournez à droite aux feux.**
to turn	you turn	Turn right at the lights.
continuer	vous continuez	**Continuez tout droit jusqu'au rond-point.**
to continue	you continue	Continue straight on until the roundabout.
descendre	vous descendez	**Descendez la rue principale.**
to go down	you go down	Go down the main road.

If you are talking to someone you would address as **tu**, you use the **tu** form of the present tense in the same way. For **-er** verbs, you omit the **-s** at the end of the **tu** form, as shown in the examples (**tourner** and **continuer**) below.

prendre	tu prends	**Prends la première rue à gauche.**
tourner	tu tournes	**Tourne à droite près du cinéma**
continuer	tu continues	**Continue tout droit.**
descendre	tu descends	**Descends la rue.**

There are a few exceptions:

être	Tu es sage.	Sois **sage!**
to be	You are well behaved. (friendly/singular)	Be good!
	Vous êtes prudent.	Soyez **prudent(s)!**
	You are careful. (polite/plural)	Be careful!
	Nous sommes heureux.	Soyons **heureux!**
	We are happy.	Let's be happy!

avoir	Tu as un biscuit.	Aie **un biscuit.**
to have	You have a biscuit. (friendly/singular)	Have a biscuit.
	Vous avez bonne chance.	Ayez **bonne chance!**
	You have good luck. (polite/plural)	Have good luck!
	Nous avons une boum.	Ayons **une boum!**
	We're having a party.	Let's have a party!

When you use the **nous** (we) form of the present tense to create an imperative it means 'let us…' or 'let's…'

For reflexive verbs, the imperative looks like this:

Lève-toi	get up
Asseyez-vous	sit down

To make imperatives negative, simply put **ne...pas** around the command (or **n'.....pas** when the verb begins with a vowel).

Ne tournez pas à gauche aux feux.
Don't turn left at the traffic lights.

? Test Yourself!

Here are some instructions. Match each one to the correct situation given below

1 **N'oublie pas ton parapluie.**
Don't forget your umbrella.
2 **Finis tes devoirs d'abord.**
Finish your homework first of all.
3 **Achetons des glaces.**
Let's buy some ice-creams.
4 **Couche-toi tout de suite.**
Go to bed straight away.
5 **Mets ton pullover.**
Put on your jumper.
6 **Prenez la première rue à gauche.**
Take the first road on the left.

A Il est minuit.
B Il pleut.
C Il fait froid.
D Il fait si chaud!
E Je peux regarder la télé?
F Pour aller au jardin public, s'il vous plaît?

Un voyage / A journey

L'année dernière, je suis allé(e)... Last year, I went...	**en Ecosse / en France / aux Etats-Unis / à Londres.** to Scotland / to France / to America / to London.
J'ai voyagé... I travelled...	**en voiture / par le train / en autocar / en bateau / en avion.** by car / by train / by coach / by boat / by plane.
Je suis parti(e) à... I set off at...	**huit heures du matin / vers midi / dix heures du soir.** 8am / about midday / 10pm.
Le voyage a duré... The journey lasted...	**une heure / environ deux heures / plus de cinq heures / une journée entière.** an hour / about 2 hours / more than 5 hours / a whole day.
A mon avis, c'était... In my opinion, it was...	**intéressant / agréable / ennuyeux / fatigant / trop long.** interesting / pleasant / boring / tiring / too long.
Pendant le voyage... During the journey...	**j'ai lu un livre / j'ai écouté mon walkman / j'ai mangé un sandwich / j'ai joué...** I read a book / I listened to my walkman / I ate a sandwich / I played...
Je suis arrivé(e)... I arrived...	**de bonne heure / à l'heure / en retard.** in good time (early) / on time / late.

L'année dernière, je suis allée à Londres avec mes parents. J'ai voyagé par le train. Pendant le voyage, j'ai mangé un pique-nique, j'ai lu un magazine et j'ai écouté de la musique. Le train est arrivé à l'heure, et j'ai trouvé le voyage agréable et confortable.

L'année dernière, je suis allé en Espagne avec ma famille. J'ai voyagé en avion. On est partis de l'aéroport à cinq heures du matin! Malheureusement, l'avion avait du retard et le voyage était long et barbant. Enfin, je suis arrivé en Espagne, mais en route pour l'hôtel, l'autocar est tombé en panne.

Exam Practice

Clémentine and Anton are talking about journeys they have made.
1. Who enjoyed the journey?
2. Who did not have a good journey?
3. Who travelled by train?
4. Who travelled by plane?

Keywords

un jour férié
bank holiday

les grandes vacances
summer holidays

une fête
festival

une fête foraine
fair

la vieille ville
the old town

un monument (historique)
(historical) sight / monument

un museé
museum

un château
castle

une cathédrale
cathedral

un parc d'attractions
theme park

A l'office du tourisme/At the tourist office

Pouvez-vous me donner …?	Can you give me …?
Avez-vous …?	Have you got …?
… un plan de la ville	… a map of the town
… une liste des restaurants	… a list of restaurants
… une liste des campings	… a list of campsites
… une liste des hôtels	… a list of hotels
… un dépliant sur les monuments	… a leaflet on the monuments
… un horaire des trains	… a train timetable
… une brochure sur la ville	… a brochure on the town
… un horaire des bus	… a bus timetable
Où est-ce que je peux manger en ville?	Where can I eat in town?
A quelle heure est-ce que le château est ouvert?	What time does the castle open?

Ecrivez à l'office du tourisme/ How to write to a tourist office

Je m'appelle…	My name is…
Je vais passer quelques jours dans votre ville au mois de…	I'm going to spend a few days in your town in … [insert month]
Je vous demande de bien vouloir m'envoyer…	Please could you send me …
Pouvez-vous me dire s'il y a…?	Can you tell me if there is / are …?
Mon adresse est…	My address is…
Je vous remercie d'avance.	Thank you in advance.

 Helpful Hint

When writing to somewhere like the tourist office, you should always use **vous** (rather than **tu**) to be polite e.g. use **Avez-vous…?** not **As tu…?**

? Test Yourself!

1 Ask what time the bus goes to the swimming pool.
2 Ask what time the museum opens.
3 Ask where you can go shopping in the town centre.

Task

Using the information on this page, write to a French tourist office and request some leaflets and brochures.

Tourism

Quel temps fait-il?/What is the weather like?

la météo	weather forecast	**il neige**	it's snowing
les prévisions	forecasts	**il fait du soleil**	it's sunny
le temps	the weather	**ensoleillé**	sunny
il fait beau	it's fine	**un orage**	a storm
il fait du brouillard	it's foggy	**il pleut**	it's raining
il fait chaud	it's hot	**la pluie**	rain
il fait froid	it's cold	**pluvieux**	rainy
il gèle	it's freezing	**du tonnerre**	thunder
il fait mauvais	it's bad weather	**des éclairs**	lightning
nuageux	cloudy	**il fait du vent**	windy

Future Tense

il va faire du soleil
it's going to be sunny

il va faire du brouillard
it's going to be foggy

il va faire froid
it's going to be cold

il va faire du vent
it's going to be windy
il va pleuvoir
it's going to rain

Past Tense

il a fait beau
it was fine

il a fait chaud
it was hot

il a plu
it rained

il a neigé
it snowed

il y a eu un orage
there was a storm

? Test Yourself!

Complete the sentences to give the weather
forecast for the five regions of France:

1. **Dans le nord,...**
2. **Dans le sud,...**
3. **Dans l'ouest,...**
4. **Dans l'est,...**
5. **Dans le centre,...**

Quelles vacances préférez-vous? What kind of holidays do you prefer?	J'aime aller en vacances au bord de la mer/ à la campagne/à la montagne/sur une île/ au bord d'un lac/en ville. I like going on holiday to the seaside/to the countryside/ to the mountains/to an island/by a lake/to a city.
Avec qui? Who with?	J'aime partir avec ma famille/mes amis/mon école. I like going away with my family/friends/school.
Quand? When?	Je préfère partir au printemps/en été/ en automne/en hiver pendant une semaine/ quinze jours/un weekend. I prefer going in spring/summer/autumn/winter for a week/15 days (a fortnight)/a weekend.
Logement? Accommodation?	Je préfère rester dans un hôtel/un appartement/ un camping/une caravane/un gîte. I prefer to stay in a hotel/an apartment/a campsite/ a caravan/a holiday home.
Activités? Activities?	J'aime bronzer à la plage/me relaxer/ visiter des monuments/faire du sport. I like sunbathing on the beach/relaxing/ visiting the sights/doing sport.

Grammaire (Perfect Tense I)

To talk about a holiday that you've been on, you need to use the *perfect tense*. The perfect tense is used to describe actions in the past, which took place within a specific time limit and are now complete.

For most verbs, to form the perfect tense you use the past participle and put **avoir**, in the present tense, in front of it. For verbs ending in **-er** the past participle is formed by taking off the **-er** and replacing it with -é.

VERB	PAST PARTICIPLE	PERFECT TENSE	
jouer (to play)	**joué**	**J'ai joué**	I played
		Tu as joué	You played
		Il/elle a joué	He/she played
		Nous avons joué	We played
		Vous avez joué	You played
		Ils/elles ont joué	They played

Here are some useful holiday activities in the perfect tense:

J'ai voyagé	I travelled	**J'ai nagé**	I swam
J'ai bronzé	I sunbathed	**J'ai joué**	I played
J'ai visité	I visited	**J'ai mangé**	I ate
J'ai acheté	I bought	**J'ai dansé**	I danced

Grammaire (Perfect Tense II)

Here are some verbs that do not end in **-er** in the perfect tense:

boire	(to drink)	**J'ai bu**	I drank
faire	(to do)	**J'ai fait**	I did
voir	(to see)	**J'ai vu**	I saw
avoir	(to have)	**J'ai eu**	I had

A small number of common verbs use **être** (to be) with the past participle, instead of **avoir**, to form the perfect tense e.g. **aller** (to go).

Je suis allé(e)	I went	**Nous sommes allé(e)s**	We went
Tu es allé(e)	You went	**Vous êtes allé(e)(s)(es)**	You went
Il est allé	He went	**Ils sont allés**	They went
Elle est allée	She went	**Elles sont allées**	They went

With these verbs, the past participle has a masculine and feminine form, which must agree with the gender of the pronoun. This means a boy would write **je suis allé** and a girl would have to write **je suis allée**.

Here are some more verbs that use **être**:

Je suis arrivé(e)	I arrived	**Je suis resté(e)**	I stayed
Je suis rentré(e)	I came home	**Je suis retourné(e)**	I returned
Je suis parti(e)	I set off	**Je suis sorti(e)**	I went out

? Test Yourself!

Write out the sentences below using the correct option from those provided.

1. **Je suis** arrivé / arriver / arrivez **à midi.**
2. **Hélène est** resté / restée / rester **dans un camping.**
3. **Nous avons** mangé / mangée / manger **dans un restaurant italien.**
4. **J'ai** nager / nagez / nagé **dans la mer.**
5. **Les deux filles sont** allé / allés / allées **en ville pour faire du shopping.**

Exam Practice

Monsieur Blanc
Je suis allé à Londres tout seul. J'ai voyagé sur la M1 en voiture - une Mini. Je suis resté dans un petit hôtel sale et inconfortable. J'ai fait une promenade en bateau et je suis tombé dans la rivière. J'ai mangé dans un restaurant londonien, mais je suis tombé malade ensuite. Le temps était froid et pluvieux.

Monsieur Bleu
Je suis allé à Blackpool avec mes amis. J'ai voyagé au bord de la mer en camping-car. Je suis resté dans un camping. J'ai visité un parc d'attractions qui s'appelle «The Pleasure Beach». J'ai mangé du poisson-frites. Je suis allé sur la plage, mais je n'ai pas nagé dans la mer. C'est trop froide. J'ai acheté un chapeau et des bonbons.

Monsieur Rouge
Je suis allé en Suisse avec ma famille. J'ai voyagé en avion privé. Je suis resté dans un hôtel de luxe avec une belle vue sur les Alpes. J'ai fait du ski. J'ai posé pour des photographes de presse devant l'hôtel. J'ai acheté une nouvelle montre en or et une pendule à coucou. Il a neigé tous les jours.

1. Read the descriptions carefully and then answer the following questions:
   - One of these holiday-makers is a celebrity. Which one do you think it is and why?
   - Who had a dreadful holiday?
   - Who went to the seaside?
   - Who was ill and why?
   - Who didn't swim and why?
   - What was bought in Switzerland?

2. Using these descriptions as a model, write an account of a holiday you have been on in the perfect tense. Include details of where you went, how you got there, who you went with, where you stayed, what the weather was like and what activities you did.

Keywords

l'agence de voyages
travel agent

l'auberge de jeunesse
youth hostel

le camping
campsite

l'hôtel
hotel

complet
full (no vacancies)

une chambre
a room

un emplacement
a space/pitch (on a campsite)

loger
to place

des arrhes
deposit

par nuit / personne
per night/person

pension complète
full board

demi-pension
half board

un parking
car park

garer
to park

eau potable
drinking water

eau non potable
not drinking water

une clef / une clé
a key

une brosse à dents
a toothbrush

du dentifrice
toothpaste

du savon
soap

un drap
a sheet

une serviette
towel

Useful Phrases

Avez-vous une chambre de libre? Je voudrais une chambre pour une personne avec une salle de bains. C'est combien, par nuit?
Have you a room free? I'd like a room for one person with a bath. How much is it per night?

Je voudrais une chambre de famille avec douche. Je voudrais rester pour une semaine. A quelle heure est le petit-déjeuner?
I would like a family room with a shower. I'd like to stay for one week. What time is breakfast?

Je voudrais une chambre avec grand lit. Je voudrais rester pour deux nuits. Ma chambre est à quel étage? Pouvez-vous me réveiller à huit heures?
I would like a room with a double bed. I'd like to stay for 2 nights. What floor is my room on? Can you wake me up at 8 o'clock?

Les chiens sont admis? Bon! Je voudrais une chambre à deux lits. Où est-ce que je peux garer ma voiture? Où est le restaurant le plus proche?
Are dogs allowed? Good! I would like a twin room. Where can I park my car? Where's the nearest restaurant?

(?) Test Yourself!

How would you ask for...?
1 ...a double room with a bath for three nights.
2 ...a single room with a shower for a week.
3 ...a family room with a bath for 2 nights.
4 ...a twin room with a shower for 2 weeks.

Accommodation

Au camping / On the campsite

Je voudrais réserver un emplacement.	I'd like to reserve a camping space.
C'est pour deux adultes et deux enfants.	It's for two adults and two children.
Nous avons une tente et une voiture.	We have a tent and a car.
Nous avons une caravane.	We have a caravan.
Il y a une piscine?	Is there a swimming pool?
On peut acheter des plats à emporter?	Can you buy take-away dishes?
On peut louer des vélos?	Can you hire bikes?
Les chiens ne sont pas admis.	Dogs are not allowed.
une salle de jeux	games room
un magasin	shop
un terrain de jeux	games area
un bloc sanitaire	washrooms
les douches	showers
les sacs de couchage	sleeping bags
une canne à pêche	fishing rod

 Task

Here is a letter of reservation to a campsite. Underline the correct option in each line, so that it contains the following information:

You want a space for three nights, from the 23rd to the 26th July, for two adults and four children. You want to hire bikes and don't want a space too near to the washrooms.

16 Irving Terrace
Birstall
Bradford
BD17 6LA

Madame,

Je voudrais un emplacement pour deux/ trois/quatre nuits, s'il vous plaît. Nous arrivons le vingt-deux juillet/ le vingt-trois juillet / le vingt-trois juin. Nous partons le vingt-six juin/ le vingt-sixjuillet/le vingt-sept juillet.

C'est pour deux adultes et deux/ trois/quatre enfants. On peut louer des vélos/des sacs de couchage/des cannes à pêche? Nous voulons un emplacement qui n'est pas près du magasin/terrain de jeux/bloc sanitaire.

Simon Johnson

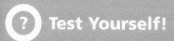 **Test Yourself!**

How would you say ...?

1. I would like a camping space for two adults and three children.
2. I have a caravan and a car.
3. Is there a shop?
4. Can I hire a tent?
5. Are dogs allowed?

Grammaire (Vouloir and Pouvoir)

The verbs **vouloir** (to want) and **pouvoir** (to be able) are very useful. Here they are in fu

je veux	I want	**je peux**	I am able/I can
tu veux	you want	**tu peux**	you can
il/elle veut	he/she wants	**il/elle/on peut**	he/she/one can
nous voulons	we want	**nous pouvons**	we can
vous voulez	you want	**vous pouvez**	you can
ils/elles veulent	they want	**ils/elles peuvent**	they can

Je veux **rester trois nuits.**	I want to stay for three nights.
Je peux **louer un vélo?**	Can I hire a bike?
Voulez-**vous réserver un emplacement?**	Do you want to reserve a space?
On peut **acheter des cannes à pêche?**	Can you buy fishing rods?
Pouvez-**vous me réveiller à huit heures?**	Can you wake me at 8 o'clock?

Mes vacances/My holiday

Pendant mes vacances, je suis resté(e) dans... During my holidays, I stayed in...	**un hôtel/un camping/un appartement/ une villa/une auberge de jeunesse/un gîte.** a hotel/a campsite/an apartment/ a villa/a youth hostel/a cottage.
C'était... It was...	**au bord de la mer/à la campagne/en ville.** by the sea/in the country / in town.
C'était... It was...	**moderne/confortable/joli/bien équipé/affreux/sale/tranquille.** modern/comfortable/pretty/ well-equipped/awful/dirty/quiet.
Il y avait... There was...	**une piscine/un jardin/un restaurant/ un terrain de golf.** a pool/garden/restaurant/a golf course.
Ma chambre avait... My room had...	**une belle vue/une douche.** a lovely view/a shower.

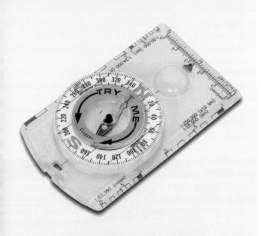

Keywords

le sous-sol	basement	**la laverie-buanderie**	laundry
le rez-de-chaussée	ground floor	**la salle de séjour**	lounge
le premier étage	first floor	**la salle de jeux**	games room
le deuxième étage	second floor	**la salle de télévision**	TV room
l'ascenseur	lift / elevator	**les toilettes (les WC)**	toilets
l'escalier	stairs	**le dortoir de garçons**	boys' dormitory
le balcon	balcony	**le dortoir des filles**	girls' dormitory
le couloir	corridor	**les douches des garçons**	boys' showers
la réception	reception	**les douches des filles**	girls' showers
la cuisine	kitchen	**une vue sur la mer**	a sea view
le réfectoire	dining room		

Task

Write a short description of the accommodation on your last holiday, using the information in this section to help you.

Accommodation

Une lettre de réservation / A letter of reservation

 Task

Write your own letter of reservation, changing the details underlined. You would like a double room with a bath for 5 nights, from the 5th to 10th August. You are arriving by train and want to know where the nearest station is.

> 13 Newtown Street
> Trafford
> Manchester
> M25 1HU
> le 4 mars
>
> Monsieur, Madame,
>
> Je voudrais réserver une chambre à votre hôtel. Je voudrais une chambre pour deux personnes avec douche pour trois nuits à partir du 14 juillet jusqu'au 17 juillet. Je vais arriver en voiture. Pouvez-vous me dire où se trouve le parking le plus proche de votre hôtel?
>
> Merci à l'avance. Je vous prie d'agréer mes sentiments les meilleurs.
>
> *Patrick Lauren*

Des problèmes / Problems

La télévision ne marche pas.
The TV doesn't work.
L'ascenseur est en panne.
The lift's out of order.
Il n'y a pas de serviettes dans ma chambre.
There are no towels in my room.
Le radiateur ne marche pas.
The radiator isn't working.
Il n'y a pas d'eau chaude.
There's no hot water.
Les draps sont sales.
The sheets are dirty.
La chambre est trop bruyante.
The room is too noisy.
Je ne peux pas ouvrir la fenêtre.
I can't open the window.
Le lit n'est pas confortable.
The bed's not comfortable.

Exam Practice

1. From the descriptions below, choose a hotel for the following people:
   - A honeymoon couple, who want to relax in comfort.
   - A sporty family, who enjoy the seaside.
   - A dog owner who wants to save money.

2. Match the correct name to each hotel.
   - HOTEL DE LA PLAGE
   - HOTEL TERMINUS
   - L'AUBERGE DE LA FORÊT

Hotel 1

★★★

Cet hôtel trois étoiles se trouve au bord de la mer à deux minutes à pied de la côte Atlantique. Il y a une piscine chauffée, un terrain de golf, des courts de tennis, un gymnase. Pour les enfants, il y a une grande salle de jeux. Chambres avec vue sur la mer. Ascenseur. Restaurant et self-service.

Hotel 2

★★★★

Notre hôtel quatre étoiles se trouve dans le calme et la verdure rurale à dix kilomètres du centre-ville. L'hôtel est entouré d'arbres et le jardin magnifique est superbe. Cadre rustique et romantique. Restaurant intime.

Hotel 3

★★

En plein centre-ville à deux minutes de la gare, l'hôtel deux étoiles offre le confort à des prix intéressants. Il n'y a pas de restaurant, mais on peut manger dans les nombreux restaurants dans le quartier. Les chiens sont acceptés. Chambres avec cabinet de toilette, dans un cadre simple mais propre.

Grammaire (Useful Verbs)

Here are some verbs which are useful when talking about holiday activities:

Dans le passé...	In the past...	A l'avenir...	In the future...
Je suis allé(e)	I went	Je vais aller	I'm going to go
Je suis parti(e)	I set off	Je vais partir	I'm going to set off
J'ai voyagé	I travelled	Je vais voyager	I'm going to travel
Je suis resté(e)	I stayed	Je vais rester	I'm going to stay
J'ai bronzé	I sunbathed	Je vais bronzer	I'm going to sunbathe
J'ai visité	I visited	Je vais visiter	I'm going to visit
J'ai acheté	I bought	Je vais acheter	I'm going to buy
J'ai nagé	I swam	Je vais nager	I'm going to swim
J'ai joué	I played	Je vais jouer	I'm going to play
J'ai mangé	I ate	Je vais manger	I'm going to eat
J'ai bu	I drank	Je vais boire	I'm going to drink
J'ai dansé	I danced	Je vais danser	I'm going to dance

 Task

1. Use the verbs alongside to write 12 complete sentences about your holiday last year (past tense).
   e.g. **L'année dernière, je suis allé en Italie. Je suis parti le dix août...**
   Last year, I went to Italy. I set off on the 10th August...

2. Now write about your plans for your next holiday (future tense).
   e.g. **En été / L'année prochaine, je vais rester dans un hôtel...**
   In the summer / Next year, I am going to stay in a hôtel...

L'année dernière, je suis allé en Espagne. Je suis parti le neuf août et je suis rentré deux semaines plus tard. J'ai voyagé en avion. Pendant le vol, j'ai écouté de la musique et j'ai lu un magazine. Je suis resté dans un grand appartement au bord de la mer. J'ai nagé dans la piscine, j'ai visité des monuments et j'ai joué au volleyball à la plage. Le soir, j'ai mangé dans un restaurant espagnol. J'ai dansé en boîte. Il a fait très chaud.

Il y a deux ans, je suis allée dans les Alpes pour faire du ski. Je suis partie en février et j'ai passé une semaine dans les Alpes françaises. J'ai voyagé en car. C'était long et fatigant. Je suis restée dans un petit hôtel. Pendant le jour, j'ai fait du ski ou j'ai fait des promenades. Le soir, je suis allée dans un bar où j'ai bu du vin rouge. Il a fait très froid et il a neigé beaucoup.

Exam Practice

Isabelle and Paul are talking about their holidays.

1. Who went to France?
2. Who went in winter?
3. Who went in summer?
4. Who had a two week holiday?
5. Who went by coach?
6. Who went swimming?
7. Who stayed in a hotel?
8. Who did not enjoy the journey?

Holiday Activities

Keywords

les fruits	fruits
un abricot	apricot
un ananas	pineapple
une banane	banana
une cerise	cherry
un citron	lemon
une fraise	strawberry
une framboise	raspberry
une pêche	peach
une poire	pear
une pomme	apple
du raisin	grapes

les légumes	vegetables
des crudités	raw vegetables
des haricots verts	green beans
une carotte	carrot
un champignon	mushroom
un chou	cabbage
un chou-fleur	cauliflower
des petits pois	peas
une pomme de terre	potato
la salade	salad
une tomate	tomato

les viandes	meats
l'agneau	lamb
les escargots	snails
le bifteck / steak	steak
le bœuf	beef
les fruits de mer	seafood
le jambon	ham
le poisson	fish
le porc	pork
le poulet	chicken
la saucisse	sausage
le saucisson	dry sausage (e.g. salami)

les boissons	drinks
la bière	beer
le cidre	cider
l'eau minérale	mineral water
la limonade	lemonade
le vin (rouge / blanc)	wine (red/white)

les desserts	desserts
le chocolat	chocolate
la confiture	jam
la crème	cream
la crêpe	pancake
le gâteau	cake
la glace	ice cream
les parfums	flavours
le sucre	sugar

d'autres aliments	other foods
le beurre	butter
un croque-monsieur	toasted sandwich
les frites	chips
le fromage	cheese
la moutarde	mustard
l'œuf	egg
l'omelette	omelette
le pain / la baguette	bread
les pâtes	pasta
le poivre	pepper
le potage	soup
le riz	rice
le sel	salt
un plat du jour	dish of the day
un plat local	local dish
les spécialitiés de la région	regional specialities
un menu à prix fixe	fixed price menu

? Test Yourself!

Choose a three course meal from the menu **(La Carte)** for...

1. ...a vegetarian.
2. ...someone with an allergy to chocolate who only eats white meat and fish.
3. ...a red-meat loving chocolate addict.

La Carte

Jambon cru	Steak-frites	Glace à la fraise
Soupe de poisson	Poulet rôti	Tarte aux framboises
Crudités	Omelette au fromage	Gâteau au chocolat

Helpful Hint

The French for *some* can be **du**, **de la** or **des** depending on the nature of the word e.g. if the word is masculine, feminine, singular or plural.

e.g. **le fromage** is masculine singular, so *some* cheese is **du fromage**
la crème is feminine singular, so *some* cream is **de la crème**
les frites is feminine plural, so *some* chips is **des frites**
les fruits is masculine plural, so *some* fruit is **des fruits**

If the word is singular and begins with a vowel, use **de l'**

e.g. **de l'eau minérale** mineral water

When you are giving the flavour or filling of a product in French this comes after the noun. The French for chocolate ice cream is **une glace au chocolat**. Use **au** for masculine singular, **à la** for feminine singular, **à l'** before vowels (singular) and **aux** before plural words.

e.g. **une omelette au fromage**
un yaourt à l'ananas
une glace à la framboise
une tarte aux cerises

? Test Yourself!

1. How would you say in French...?
...some cherries
...some strawberries
...some mustard
...some lemonade
...some salt
...a cheese sandwich
...a coffee cake
...a strawberry yoghurt
...apricot jam

2. Use the endings provided to complete the sentences below.
- **Je voudrais une table pour...**
- **Pour commencer, je prends...**
- **Comme plat principal, on prend...**
- **Comme dessert, je voudrais...**
- **Monsieur, on a fini de manger, je voudrais...**
- deux poissons.
- l'addition, s'il vous plaît.
- deux personnes.
- une soupe à l'oignon.
- deux glaces à la vanille.

Useful Phrases

Je voudrais réserver une table pour deux personnes.
I'd like to reserve a table for two.

La carte, s'il vous plaît.
The menu, please.

J'ai besoin d'un couteau / une fourchette / une cuiller / une assiett
I need a knife / fork / spoon / plate.

Le verre / la tasse est sale.
The glass / cup is dirty.

Le garçon / la serveuse.
The waiter / waitress.

Pour commencer, je prends...
To start, I'll have...

Le plat du jour, c'est quoi?
What is the dish of the day?

Voici un pourboire.
Here's a tip.

L'addition, s'il vous plaît.
The bill, please.

Le service est compris / n'est pas compris.
Service included / not included.

Holiday Activities

Grammaire (Negatives)

To form a negative, you put **ne...pas** around the verb
(**n'...pas** if the verb begins with a vowel).

Je ne **mange** pas **de viande**	I don't eat meat
Je n'**aime** pas **le vin**	I don't like wine

In the perfect tense, you make the correct form of **avoir** or **être** negative.

Je suis allé au restaurant	I went to the restaurant
Je ne **suis** pas **allé au restaurant**	I didn't go to the restaurant
J'ai acheté une glace	I bought an ice cream
Je n'**ai** pas **acheté de glace**	I didn't buy an ice cream

After a negative, **un**, **une**, **du**, **de la** and **des** all change to **de**.

Other negative expressions:

ne...plus	no longer / no more
ne...rien	nothing
ne...jamais	never
ne ...personne	nobody

Je ne **mange** plus **de frites**	I don't eat chips any more
Je n'**aime** rien **sur le menu**	I don't like anything on the menu
Je ne **mange** jamais **de porc**	I never eat pork
Personne n'**a mangé le poisson**	Nobody ate the fish

Task

Now try to write the following phrases in French:

1. I eat nothing in the morning
2. I don't eat steak
3. I don't drink beer any more
4. I never eat cheese
5. Nobody likes mushrooms
6. I've never eaten seafood

 Exam Practice

 Paul

En vacances, j'ai mangé dans un petit restaurant italien où j'ai choisi des pâtes pour commencer et puis j'ai mangé une pizza aux fruits de mer. Comme dessert, j'ai pris une glace au chocolat. C'était délicieux. Le service était excellent et ce n'était pas très cher. On a très bien mangé.

Restaurant Italien

 **Isabelle**

En vacances, j'ai mangé dans un restaurant espagnol. J'ai choisi une salade, mais j'ai trouvé une limace dans mon assiette. J'ai commandé une omelette, mais c'était horrible. Je n'ai pas pris de dessert, parce que je ne voulais plus manger. Le café était froid. On a expliqué à la serveuse, mais elle n'a rien dit. En plus, le repas était très cher. Quelle catastrophe!

Restaurant Espagnol

Read the two accounts of restaurant meals above:

1. Who had an unpleasant experience? Explain why?
2. Who enjoyed the meal? Say what they had to eat.

Clue: **une limace** = a slug

Keywords

une boîte aux lettres	letter box	mettre à la poste	to post
une carte postale	postcard	une lettre	letter
un paquet	parcel	un timbre	stamp
une caisse	a till	une cabine téléphonique	phone box
une télécarte	phone card	la tonalité	dialling tone
le numéro	number	décrocher	to pick up the receiver
raccrocher	to hang up		

A la banque / At the bank

Je voudrais changer de l'argent.	I'd like to change some money.
Je voudrais changer un chèque de voyage.	I'd like to change a travellers cheque.
Quel est le taux de change?	What's the exchange rate?
Il y a une commission?	Is there a commission charge?
une livre sterling	a British pound

A la poste / At the Post Office

Je voudrais envoyer une carte postale en Italie.	I'd like to send a postcard to Italy.
Je voudrais envoyer une lettre au Pays de Galles.	I'd like to send a letter to Wales.
Je voudrais envoyer un paquet aux Etats-Unis.	I'd like to send a parcel to the USA.
C'est combien, s'il vous plaît?	How much does it cost, please?

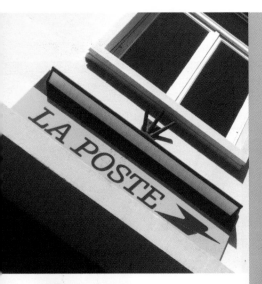

 Helpful Hint

masculine countries
e.g. **le Canada, le Pays de Galles**
au **Canada,** au **Pays de Galles**

feminine countries
e.g. **la Grande-Bretagne, l'Angleterre**
en **Grande-Bretagne,** en **Angleterre**

plural countries
e.g. **les Etats-Unis**
aux **Etats-Unis**

 Task

Here are some instructions for using a French pay phone. Using the information on this page to help you, put the English instructions below into the correct order.

- **Introduisez votre télécarte.**
- **Décrochez le combiné.**
- **Attendez la tonalité.**
- **Composez le numéro.**
- **A la fin de l'appel, raccrochez.**
- **Retirez votre télécarte.**

- Dial the number.
- Take out your phone card.
- Insert your phone card.
- Lift the receiver.
- Hang up when finished.
- Wait for the dialling tone.

? Test Yourself!

How would you say you'd like to...?
1 ...send a postcard to England.
2 ...send a postcard to Wales.
3 ...send a letter to America.
4 ...send a letter to Canada.
5 ...send a parcel to Scotand.
6 ...send a parcel to Italy.

Au bureau des objects trouvés / At the lost property office

J'ai perdu...	I've lost...
J'ai laissé...	I left...
On m'a volé...	I've had stolen...
mon parapluie	my umbrella
ma valise	my suitcase
mes lunettes	my glasses
mon portefeuille	my wallet
ma montre	my watch
mes bagages	my luggage
mon porte-monnaie	my purse
ma bague	my ring
mes gants	my gloves
mon passeport	my passport
ma clef	my key
mes bijoux	my jewellery
mon sac à main	my handbag
mon appareil-photo	my camera
dans la rue	in the street
dans le parc	in the park
à la gare	at the station
dans le train	on the train
dans le bus	on the bus
à l'hôtel	at the hotel
au café	in the cafe
au restaurant	at the restaurant

C'est noir / marron / grand / petit
It's black / brown / big / small
En cuir / en argent / en or
It's made of leather / silver / gold
Il y a cent euros dedans
There are 100 euros inside

Exam Practice

Read the dialogue and then answer the questions below.

- **Bonjour! Quel est le taux de change de la livre sterling?**
- Un euro trente, madame.
- **Je voudrais changer dix livres.**
- Ça fait treize euros, mais il y a une commission de deux euros. Vous recevrez donc onze euros en tout.

1. What is the exchange rate?
2. How much currency does the customer want to change?
3. How much is the commission?

Louer / To hire

Je voudrais louer...	I'd like to hire...
un vélo	a bike
un VTT	a mountain bike
une planche à voile	a windsurf board
un sac de couchage	a sleeping bag
un canot	a rowing boat
un transat	a deckchair

C'est combien par heure / par jour?
How much is it per hour / per day?

? Test Yourself!

How would you report these losses?
1. You've lost your brown, leather wallet in the street.
2. You left your black umbrella on the bus.
3. You've had your passport stolen.
4. You've lost your handbag. It's a small, leather bag with 50 euros inside.

Chez le médecin / At the doctor's

un dentiste	dentist
une infirmière	nurse
un médecin / docteur	doctor
une pharmacie	pharmacy

Les parties du corps / Parts of the body

la bouche	mouth
le bras	arm
le cou	neck
la dent	tooth
le doigt	finger
le dos	back
l'épaule	shoulder
l'estomac / le ventre	stomach
le genou	knee
la gorge	throat
la jambe	leg
la main	hand
le nez	nose
l'œil / les yeux	eye / eyes
l'oreille	ear
le pied	foot
la tête	head

Les symptômes / Symptoms

couper	to cut
casser	to break
une éruption	a rash
une fièvre	a fever
un rhume	a cold
vomir	to vomit

Je ne peux pas dormir	I can't sleep
J'ai perdu l'appétit, j'ai mal au cœur	I've lost my appetite, I have nausea
Je suis enrhumé, j'ai la grippe	I've caught cold, I've got 'flu
Je suis malade, j'ai de la fièvre	I am ill, I have a temperature
J'ai mal au pied / à la gorge	I have a sore foot / a sore throat
J'ai mal à l'estomac / aux dents	I have a stomach ache / tooth ache

Helpful Hint

Use **avoir** not **être** in the following expressions:

J'ai froid	I'm cold
J'ai chaud	I'm hot
J'ai faim	I'm hungry
J'ai soif	I'm thirsty
but	
Je suis fatigué(e)	I'm tired

Test Yourself!

Pick an expression from those above to match each of the following statements:

e.g. **Je suis fatigué.**

Je ne peux pas dormir

1 j'ai un rhume.
2 j'ai envie de vomir.
3 je ne me sens pas bien.
4 je ne veux pas manger.

Services

A la pharmacie / At the pharmacy

Avez-vous...?	have you...?	**des comprimés**	tablets
de l'aspirine	aspirin	**une crème solaire**	sun cream
des pastilles	throat pastilles	**un médicament**	medicine
du sparadrap	plasters	**des mouchoirs en papier**	tissues

Des problèmes et des accidents / Problems and accidents

les premiers soins	first aid
une ceinture de sécurité	safety belt
les sapeurs-pompiers	fire brigade
une ambulance	ambulance
un hôpital	hospital
la mort	death
au secours!	help!
la police	police
un gendarme	policeman
blessé	injured
heurter	to collide
tuer	to kill
un incendie	fire
grave	serious
sérieusement	seriously

Obtenir l'aide / getting help

In most European countries, including France, you dial 112 for the emergency services.

- **J'ai eu un accident dans ma voiture. Un chien a traversé la route en courant. J'ai évité le chien, mais j'ai heurté un arbre.**
  I've had an accident in my car. A dog ran across the road. I avoided the dog, but hit a tree.
- **Vous êtes où exactement?**
  Where are you exactly?
- **Je suis sur la route nationale 20 à deux kilomètres de Guéret.**
  I'm on the N20, two kilometres from Guéret.
- **Vous êtes blessé?**
  Are you injured?
- **J'ai mal au cou.**
  I've a sore neck.
- **Je vais alerter la police et je vais envoyer une ambulance tout de suite.**
  I'll inform the police and send an ambulance straight away.

Le Monde

Accident De Route

Un accident grave s'est passé hier soir sur la route national 20, quand une voiture est entré en collison avec un autobus. Le conducteur de la Renault a été sérieusement blessé. Il a été transporté à l'hôpital de Limoges en hélicoptère. Sa condition reste stable, mais il va rester à l'hôpital pour l'instant. Selon la police, le conducteur ne portait pas de ceinture de sécurité.

Incendie dans un Appartment

Un incendie a détruit un appartement au centre-ville hier après-midi. Les sapeurs-pompiers ont dit qu'une ciga-rette a provoqué un feu dans le salon Hereusement, per-sonne n'a été blessé.

Jeune Fille Blessée

Une jeune fille de 13 ans, qui jouait au foot dans une équipe pour filles, a été blessée au bras. Ses adversaires jouaient un peu trop agressivement. Une ambu-lance l'a transportée à l'hôpital où elle a reçu les premiers soins. Elle est rentrée à la maison deux heures après.

Cycliste Blessé

Un jeune garçon de 14 ans a été blessé lundi matin quand un camion a heurté son vélo au centre-ville près de la gare. Le jeune s'est cassé la jambe droite.

Exam Practice

Read the newspaper reports alongside.
1. Which article is about a sporting injury?
2. Which article is about a fire?
3. Which article is about a serious road accident?
4. Which article is about a cycling accident?

In more detail...

'Incendie dans un Appartement'
5. When did the incident take place?
6. What caused it?

'Accident De Route'
7. What exactly happened?
8. Where is the injured man now?
9. What possibly made the injuries worse?

'Cycliste Blessé'
10. Where and when did the accident happen?
11. What was the result?

'Jeune Fille Blessée'
12. What caused the accident?
13. Where is the girl now?

Grammaire

The verbs **faire** (to do) and **mettre** (to put on) are irregular. Make sure you know how to use them correctly to talk about different people.

je fais **les courses**
I do the shopping
mon père fait **le repassage**
my father does the ironing
nous faisons **la vaisselle**
we do the washing up
mes parents font **le ménage**
my parents do the housework

je mets **la table**
I set the table
il met **la table**
he sets the table
mon frère et moi mettons **la table**
my brother and I set the table
ils mettent **la table**
they are setting the table

Les corvées / The chores

faire la cuisine	to do the cooking
faire les courses	to go shopping (for groceries)
faire le jardinage	to do the gardening
faire le ménage	to do the housework
faire le repassage	to do the ironing
faire la vaisselle	to do the washing up
laver les fenêtres / la voiture	to wash the windows / the car
débarrasser la table	to clear the table
mettre la table / le couvert	to set the table
passer l'aspirateur	to do the vacuuming
promener le chien	to walk the dog
sortir la poubelle	to put out the bin
ranger la chambre	to tidy the bedroom
nettoyer	to clean

 Helpful Hint

When answering questions about your home life and daily routine, you can make your answer more interesting by using expressions of time:

rarement	rarely
ne ... jamais	never
souvent	often
tous les jours	every day
régulièrement	regularly
généralement	usually
quelquefois	sometimes
de temps en temps	from time to time
une fois par semaine	once a week
deux fois par semaine	two times a week

e.g.

Je promène les chien tous les jours.	I walk the dog every day.
Je fais souvent la vaisselle.	I often do the washing up.
Je ne range jamais ma chambre.	I never tidy my room.

 Task

Give your opinion of each of the 14 household chores listed alongside. U the following phrases to help you:

J'adore...	I love...
J'aime bien...	I quite like...
..., ça ne me dérange pas.	..., I don't mind
..., ça va.	..., it's OK
Je n'aime pas tellement...	I don't like very much...
Je déteste...	I hate...
Je ne peux pas supporter...	I can't stand...

e.g. **Faire la lessive, ça ne me dérange pas.**
I don't mind doing the washing.
Je ne peux pas supporter faire la lessive!
I can't stand doing the washing!

Home Life

Useful Phrases

- Bon appétit! — Enjoy your meal!
- Oui, je veux bien! — Yes, please!
- Non, merci! — No, thank you!
- C'est délicieux. — It's delicious.
- Voulez-vous...? — Do you want...?
- Voulez-vous encore du gâteau? — Do you want some more cake?
- J'en ai assez mangé, merci. — I've had enough to eat, thank you.
- Je peux...? — Can I...?
- Je peux débarrasser la table? — Can I clear the table?
- Je mange souvent... — I often eat…
- Je ne mange jamais de... — I never eat…
- Je n'ai jamais goûté... — I've never tasted...
- Je voudrais essayer... — I'd like to try...
- Pouvez-vous...? — Can you...?
- Pouvez-vous me passer le sel, s'il vous plaît? — Can you pass me the salt, please?
- Pouvez-vous m'aider à faire la vaisselle? — Can you help me do the washing up?

? Test Yourself!

1. How do you...?
   - Ask if you can wash up.
   - Ask someone to pass you the bread.
   - Ask someone if they want water.
   - Accept a second helping.
   - Refuse a second helping politely.

2. What would *you* say about the following?
   - des escargots
   - des moules
   - des asperges
   - des frites
   - des sardines
   - des haricots verts
   - des cuisses de grenouille

Exam Practice

Annie: Je ne prends jamais de petit-déjeuner. Je mange à la cantine scolaire à midi. Je prends souvent une salade et un yaourt. Le soir, je dîne vers sept heures et demie avec mes parents. Je ne mange jamais de viande ni de poisson.

Morgane: Je prends des céréales au petit-déjeuner et je bois généralement du chocolat chaud. A midi, je rentre à la maison et je prends le déjeuner avec maman et ma petite sœur. Le soir, pour le dîner, je mange de la viande ou du poisson avec des légumes.

Philippe: Pour le petit-déjeuner, je prends généralement du pain grillé avec de la confiture et un jus d'orange. Je prends le petit-déjeuner dans la cuisine à sept heures. A l'heure du déjeuner, j'aime manger dans la cantine au collège. Je préfère le steak-frites. Le soir, je ne mange pas beaucoup. On dîne vers huit heures.

Read the descriptions above.
1. Who does not have breakfast?
2. Who has fruit juice at breakfast?
3. Who drinks hot chocolate?
4. Who could be a vegetarian?
5. Who goes home for lunch?
6. Who eats at 8pm?

Grammaire (Future Tense)

If you look up *to eat* in a French dictionary, you will find **manger**. This is called the *stem* of the verb. In French, with most verbs, you form the future tense by simply adding the correct ending to this stem.

Je mangerai	I will eat	**Nous manger**ons	We will eat
Tu mangeras	You will eat	**Vous manger**ez	You will eat
Il/Elle mangera	He/She will eat	**Ils/Elles manger**ont	They will eat

For verbs that end in **-re** (e.g. **cuire**, **lire**, **mettre**), remove the **-e** to form the stem before adding the endings.

Je cuirai **le dîner**	I will cook dinner
Elle lira **la recette**	She will read the recipe
Ils mettront **la table**	They will set the table

As you might expect, there are some verbs that do not follow this pattern. *All* verbs use exactly the same endings to form the future tense however, the stem sometimes has to be learned separately. Here are some of the most common irregular verbs:

être to be (the stem is ser-)
Je serai **à la maison en retard** — I will be late home

avoir to have (the stem is aur-)
Il aura **sa propre chambre** — He will have his own room

faire to do (the stem is fer-)
Tu feras **du shopping?** — Will you go shopping?

aller to go (the stem is ir-)
Nous irons **au supermarché** — We will go to the supermarket

voir to see (the stem is verr-)
Vous verrez **mon frère?** — Will you see my brother?

venir to come (the stem is viendr-)
Elles viendront **demain** — They'll come tomorrow

The future tense is used most often in written French. Another way of expressing future plans is to use **aller** + the infinitive (see page 24). This method is especially common in spoken French.

? **Test Yourself!**

Using the information on this page, choose the correct future tense for the following phrases.

1. **Mon père** ferai / fera / feront **la cuisine.**
2. **Nous** ferons / ferez / feront **les courses.**
3. **Je** débarrasserai / débarrasseras / débarrassera **la table.**
4. **Ma sœur** laverai / laveras / lavera **la voiture.**
5. **Les filles** rangerons / rangera / rangeront **la chambre.**

 Task

Which of the following chores will you do next weekend? Put them in the future tense and use the negative if necessary.

e.g. **Le week-end prochain, je ferai le ménage.**
Next weekend, I will do the housework.

or **Le week-end prochain, je ne ferai pas le ménage.**
Next weekend, I will not do the housework.

1. wash the car
2. set the table
3. do the vacuuming
4. put out the bin
5. tidy the bedroom
6. do the ironing

Home Life

Les fêtes / Festivals

chanter	to sing
fêter	to celebrate
la messe	Mass
un anniversaire	birthday
Noël	Christmas
la Saint-Sylvestre	New Year's Eve
le jour de l'an	New Year's Day
Pâques	Easter
un jour férié	Bank Holiday
le poisson d'avril	April Fools' Day
le mardi gras	Shrove Tuesday
la Fête Nationale	Bastille Day (14th July)
religieux	religious
spécial	special
un cadeau	a gift

Exam Practice

Read these descriptions of three festivals and answer the questions.

1. Which of the descriptions is in the past tense?
2. Which is written in the present?
3. Which is written in the future?
4. **Qui aime le chocolat?**
5. **Qui va boire du lait?**
6. **Qui s'intéresse à l'informatique?**

Elisa (15 ans) - J'aime beaucoup Pâques, parce que j'adore manger des œufs en chocolat. En France, les parents cachent des œufs dans le jardin et les enfants essaient de les trouver.

Ahmed (16 ans) - On va bientôt fêter l'Aïd, c'est le dernier jour du Ramadan. On boira un verre de lait et ensuite on mangera une soupe spéciale qui s'appelle la chorba. Ma mère préparera du couscous et beaucoup de petits gâteaux très sucrés.

Mathilde (14 ans) - L'année dernière, pour Noël, j'ai reçu un nouvel ordinateur de mes parents. On a mangé du pâté, de la dinde avec des légumes. Mes grands-parents sont venus chez nous et je me suis très bien amusée.

Helpful Hint

To write about an important festival...

1. Give the time of year or the date

   e.g. **Le 25 décembre, on fête Noël.**
   On the 25th December, we celebrate Christmas.
   En février, on fête le mardi gras.
   In February, we celebrate Shrove Tuesday.

2. Say what you do

   e.g. **On mange...** We eat...
   On boit... We drink...
   On offre... We give...
   On reçoit... We receive...

3. Give your opinion

   e.g. **C'est une journée très amusante.**
   It's a very enjoyable day.
   On s'amuse beaucoup.
   We have a really good time.

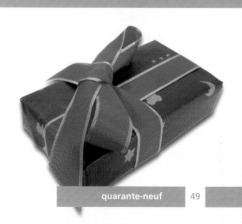

Grammaire (Prepositions)

In French, there are three different ways of saying *for* when talking about periods of time: Use **pendant** if the activity is finished and complete. Use **depuis** if the activity is still going on and is not complete. Use **pour** if the activity hasn't started yet.

e.g. **J'ai joué au football** pendant **deux heures.**
I played football *for* 2 hours.
Je joue au tennis depuis **deux ans.**
I've been playing tennis *for* 2 years.
Je vais faire du ski pour **deux jours.**
I'm going to go skiing *for* 2 days.

Pendant is usually used with the perfect tense. **Depuis** is usually used with the present tense. **Pour** is usually used with the future tense (or the present if it's expressing future intentions). Note how we translate **depuis** phrases into English.

e.g. **Je fume des cigarettes** depuis **un an.**
I've been smoking for a year.
Je fais de la voile depuis **trois ans.**
I've been going sailing for three years.
Je suis végétarien depuis **deux semaines.**
I've been vegetarian for two weeks.

These three sentences use **depuis** because the speaker is *still* a smoking, vegetarian sailor.

Useful Phrases

A mon avis, je suis en bonne forme.	In my opinion, I am fit.
Je crois que je suis en assez bonne forme.	I think I am quite fit.
J'essaie de garder la forme.	I try to stay fit.
Je garde la forme en faisant beaucoup de sport.	I keep fit by doing sport.
En général, je suis en bonne santé.	In general I am healthy.
Je ne suis pas en très bonne forme.	I'm not very fit.
Je ne fais pas beaucoup de sport.	I don't do much sport.
je suis paresseux(se).	I'm lazy.

(?) Test Yourself!

Fill in the gaps with **pendant**, **pour** or **depuis**.

1. **J'ai fait de la danse _____ trois ans, mais maintenant je préfère le sport.**
2. **Je vais faire du ski. J'irai dans les Alpes _____ deux semaines.**
3. **Je joue au rugby _____ cinq ans. C'est super.**
4. **Je suis allée au gymnase _____ deux semaines, mais je n'ai pas aimé ça.**

Healthy Living

Put the following food and drink into two columns: **Bon pour la santé** (Good for the health) or **Mauvais pour la santé** (Bad for the health).

les frites	la salade
le pain	l'eau minérale
le chocolat	les gâteaux
le coca-cola	la crème
le poisson	le poulet
les bonbons	la viande rouge
la bière	le café
le vin rouge	les céréales
le riz	le fromage
les fruits	les légumes

Tu es sportif / sportive?
Are you sporty?

Je suis... I'm...	**très sportif / assez sportive.** very sporty / quite sporty.
Je fais du sport... I do sport...	**une fois par semaine / deux fois par semaine / souvent / de temps en temps.** once a week / twice a week / often / from time to time.
Je joue au... / J'adore le... / Je déteste le... I play... / I love... / I hate...	**football / tennis / badminton / netball cricket / rugby.** football / tennis / badminton / netball / cricket / rugby.
...parce que c'est... ...because it is...	**fatigant / dangereux / difficile / violent / super / passionnant / facile / bon pour la santé.** tiring / dangerous / difficult / violent / great / exciting / easy / good for the health.

Qu'est-ce que tu aimes manger?
What do you like eating?

Je mange... I eat..	**bien / équilibré.** well / a balanced diet.
Je mange beaucoup de... / J'aime manger de... I eat a lot of... / I like eating...	**fruits / légumes / salade / poulet / poisson.** fruit / vegetables / salad / chicken / fish.
J'évite de manger... / Je suis tenté(e) par... I avoid eating... / I am tempted by...	**du chocolat / des bonbons / des gâteaux.** chocolate / sweets / cakes.
Je préfère la cuisine... I prefer...	**italienne / indienne / chinoise / anglaise.** Italian / Indian / Chinese / English food.
J'aime le... / je n'aime pas le... / Je mange trop de... I like... / I don't like... / I eat too much...	**fast-food.** fast food.

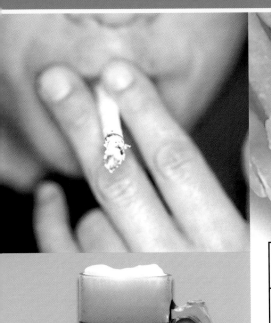
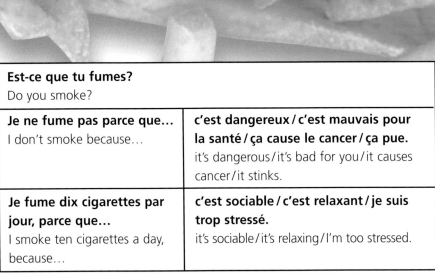

Est-ce que tu fumes? Do you smoke?	
Je ne fume pas parce que… I don't smoke because…	**c'est dangereux / c'est mauvais pour la santé / ça cause le cancer / ça pue.** it's dangerous / it's bad for you / it causes cancer / it stinks.
Je fume dix cigarettes par jour, parce que… I smoke ten cigarettes a day, because…	**c'est sociable / c'est relaxant / je suis trop stressé.** it's sociable / it's relaxing / I'm too stressed.

Tu bois de l'alcool? Do you drink alcohol?	
Je bois… I drink…	**quelquefois / de temps en temps, le weekend généralement.** sometimes / from time to time, usually at the weekend.
J'aime… I like…	**la bière / le vin rouge / le vin blanc etc.** beer / red wine / white wine etc.
Je ne bois jamais parce que… I don't drink because…	**c'est mauvais pour le foie / je n'aime pas le goût / je suis trop jeune.** it's bad for the liver / I don't like the taste / I am too young.

? Test Yourself!

In French, how do you say…?

1 I drink alcohol sometimes because it is sociable.
2 I am stressed but I don't smoke because it is bad for you.
3 I drink wine sometimes, usually with dinner.

✏ Task

The statements below are all about smoking. For each one, decide whether you think it is a smoker or non-smoker speaking.

1 **C'est relaxant.**
2 **Ça cause le cancer.**
3 **Le tabagisme passif est très dangereux pour les non-fumeurs.**
4 **Les vêtements sentent mauvais.**
5 **On a les dents jaunes.**
6 **C'est sociable quand on est avec ses amis.**
7 **C'est un bon remède contre le stress.**
8 **C'est très mauvais pour le cœur.**

Healthy Living

? Test Yourself!

Read the following sentences about healthy living. Match the correct English translation to each one and write alongside whether it uses past, present or future tense.

1. Je ne vais jamais fumer - cela cause le cancer.
2. Hier, j'ai mangé un grand gâteau au chocolat.
3. Je préfère la cuisine italienne parce que j'adore les pizzas et les pâtes.
4. Je ne fume pas parce que c'est dangereux pour les poumons.
5. Hier soir, j'ai fumé une cigarette pour me relaxer avec mes amis.
6. Je n'ai pas l'intention de boire de l'alcool parce que c'est mauvais pour la santé.
7. Je voudrais jouer au squash parce que c'est très rapide.
8. J'ai bu trois verres de vin rouge et une bouteille de bière.
9. Je vais à la piscine une fois par semaine.
10. J'irai au gymnase régulièrement quand je serai plus âgé.

A. I prefer Italian cooking because I love pizzas and pasta.
B. I go to the swimming pool once a week.
C. I don't smoke because it's dangerous for the lungs.
D. I drank three glasses of red wine and a bottle of beer.
E. Last night I smoked a cigarette to relax with friends.
F. Yesterday I ate a big chocolate cake.
G. I'll go to the gym regularly when I'm older.
H. I'm never going to smoke - it causes cancer.
I. I don't intend to drink alcohol because it's bad for you.
J. I'd like to play squash because it's very fast.

Helpful Hint

Expressions of time can help to make your descriptions far more informative (see pages 12, 46).

Je mange du fromage tous les jours.
I eat cheese everyday.
Je bois régulièrement de l'eau.
I regularly drink water.
Je fais du sport une fois par semaine.
I do sport once a week.
Je ne fume jamais de cigarettes.
I never smoke cigarettes.

Task

Write a short essay, in French, about your lifestyle. Discuss whether it is healthy or not and try to include some examples using the past tense. Here are some useful phrases to help.

- **Le weekend dernière, je suis allé au centre sportif où j'ai joué...**
  Last weekend, I went to the sports centre where I played...
- **Hier, j'ai mangé...**
  Yesterday, I ate...

Quel est ton avis?/What's your opinion?

- **Etre en bonne forme est important.** — Being fit is important
- **Cela cause des maladies.** — That causes illness.
- **Fumer est très mauvais pour la santé.** — Smoking is bad for you.
- **Les cigarettes causent le cancer.** — Cigarettes cause cancer.
- **Le tabagisme passif est dangereux.** — Passive smoking is dangerous.
- **Les jeunes consomment trop de sucre et de graisse.** — The young consume too much sugar and fat.
- **Cela cause des problèmes plus tard.** — That causes problems later on.
- **A mon avis les gens fument trop/boivent trop/ne font pas assez de sport/mangent trop de...** — In my opinion people smoke too much/drink too much/don't do enough sport/eat too much…

In the UK, it is illegal for anyone under the age of 18 to buy alcohol or consume it on licensed premises. Binge drinking and smoking both have adverse effects on your health and can lead to addictions.

Chercher le travail /
Looking for work

- **Il est difficile de trouver un bon emploi.**
  It is hard to find a good job.
- **Il y a beaucoup d'emplois dans des cafés et des hôtels.**
  There are lots of jobs available in cafes and hotels.
- **Ils ne sont pas bien payés.**
  The pay is not good.
- **Je voudrais trouver un emploi plus intéressant.**
  I would like to find a more interesting job.
- **Beaucoup de mes amis travaillent dans des restaurants.**
  A lot of my friends work in restaurants.
- **Je n'aime pas travailler le week-end parce que j'aime sortir avec mes amis.**
  I don't like working at the weekends because I like to go out with my friends.
- **Mes parents n'aiment pas que je travaille le soir parce que j'ai les devoirs.**
  My parents don't like me working in the evenings because I have homework.

 Task

Use the phrases below to write a short piece about any part-time work you do. Give information about what you do, where you do it, how you get there, working hours etc.

Useful Phrases

J'ai un petit job.	I have a part-time job.
Je livre des journaux.	I deliver newspapers.
Je fais du baby-sitting.	I go babysitting.
Je sers des clients.	I serve customers.
Je gagne... livres par jour.	I earn... pounds per day.
Je vais au travail en...	I go to work by...
Je commence le travail à... heures.	I start work at...
Je travaille... heures par jour.	I work... hours a day.
Je finis le travail à... heures	I finish work at...
Le samedi, je travaille dans un café / magasin.	On Saturdays, I work in a café / shop.

Serveur - waiter/barman   un Cassier - cashier
vendeur - salesperson

Grammaire (The Imperfect Tense)

The *perfect* tense is used to describe an action that took place in the past, which is complete and took place in a specific period of time (see pages 13, 32, 33). The *imperfect* tense is used to describe past actions that weren't completed, happened more than once (i.e. were repeated) or were ongoing over an indefinite period of time. It can often be translated as *I was doing* or *I used to do*.

e.g. **Quand j'étais petit(e), je voulais devenir médecin.**
When I was little, I used to want to be a doctor.

Here, the *imperfect* tense is used because the action (wanting to be a doctor) took place over an unspecified period of time.

e.g. **Je travaillais dans le magasin, quand mon professeur de français est arrivé.**
I was working in the shop, when my French teacher arrived.

Here the first verb is *imperfect* (I was working = interrupted action), but the second is *perfect* (teacher arrived = happened once and is complete).

To form the *imperfect* tense, you take the **nous** form of the verb in the present tense and remove the ending **–ons**. You then add the correct imperfect ending, shown below.

e.g. **travailler** to work (**nous travaillons** we work / we are working)

je travaillais	I was working/I used to work
tu travaillais	You were working
il / elle travaillait	He / She was working
nous travaillions	We were working
vous travailliez	You were working
ils / elles travaillaient	They were working

The only exception is **être** (to be). You use **ét-** as the stem, *not* the **nous** form of the present tense (**nous sommes**). However, the verb endings for the imperfect tense are exactly the same.

j'étais	I was
tu étais	You were
il / elle était	He / She was
nous étions	We were
vous étiez	You were
ils / elles étaient	They were

 Task

1 Match the correct imperfect French phrase to the following English expressions:

I used to watch	I used to wear	**J'avais...**	**J'adorais...**
I used to have	I used to hate	**Je lisais...**	**Je portais...**
I used to love	I used to drink	**Je mangeais...**	**Je détestais...**
I used to eat	I used to read	**Je regardais...**	**Je buvais...**

2 Using the verbs above, write a passage about what you were like when you were little,
e.g. **Je portais une petite robe, je buvais du lait...**

Part-Time Jobs a

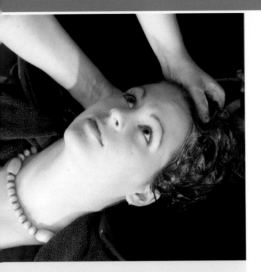

Mon stage pratique / My work experience

L'année dernière / il y a six mois, pendant quinze jours, j'ai travaillé comme... Last year / six months ago, for 15 days, I worked as...	**un(e) coiffeur(euse) / un(e) vendeur(euse) / un(e) employé(e) de bureau.** a hairdresser / a sales person / an office worker.
J'ai fait mon stage pratique dans... I did my work experience in...	**une banque / un bureau / un hôpital / une usine / une école / un magasin.** a bank / an office / a hospital / a factory / a school / a shop.
Je commençais à... / Je finissais à... I started at... / I finished at...	**huit heures / neuf heures / cinq heures.** 8 o'clock / nine o'clock / five o'clock.
J'y allais en... / Je voyageais en... I went there by... / I travelled by...	**voiture / vélo / scooter / autobus / taxi.** car / bike / scooter / bus / taxi.
Je (J')... I...	**servais les clients / aidais les enfants / photocopiais des documents / préparais du thé.** served customers / helped the children / photocopied documents / made the tea.
Dans l'ensemble, le stage était... Overall, the experience was...	**intéressant(e) / ennuyeux(euse) / amusant(e) / utile / difficile.** interesting / boring / fun / useful / difficult.
Mes collègues étaient... / Mon patron était... My colleagues were... / My boss was...	**sympa / agréeable / travailleur(euse) / paresseux(euse) / antipathique.** nice / pleasant / hard-working / lazy / unfriendly.
A l'avenir, j'ai l'intention... In the future, I intend...	**de poursuivre mes études et d'aller à l'université / d'aller voyager.** to continue my studies and go to university / to go travelling.
J'espère... / je vais... / je veux... / je voudrais... I hope... / I'm going... / I want... / I would like...	**être professeur / secrétaire / dentiste / agent de police.** to be a teacher / secretary / dentist / police officer.

Task

Using the table on this page, and the additional useful phrases on the facing page, write an account of your work experience.

d Work Experience

Helpful Hint

Try to make your descriptions as detailed and interesting as possible. Here are some more useful phrases to help you do this:

- **Pour moi, un stage pratique est important et utile parce que...**
- **Les stages pratiques sont une perte de temps parce que...**
- **J'ai décidé de travailler dans...**
- **Mon école a organisé le stage pour moi.**

- **J'ai écrit une lettre...**
- **J'ai visité... / J'ai téléphoné... / J'ai parlé avec le patron avant de commencer.**
- **Je suis allé(e) à une interview et j'ai posé des questions sur...**

- For me, work experience is important and useful because...
- Work experience placements are a waste of time because...
- I decided to work in...
- My school organised the placement for me.

- I wrote a letter...
- I visited... / I phoned.../ I spoke with the boss before starting.
- I went to an interview and I asked questions about...

Exam Practice

Here are three messages left on an answering machine. Summarise what is said in each.

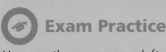

Merci de votre demande d'emploi. Pourriez-vous me téléphoner pour organiser un entretien?

Je veux savoir si tu peux travailler samedi à 10 heures. Rappelle-moi le plus vite possible.

Je vous appelle de la part de Monsieur Lebrun. Il voudrait venir vous voir mardi prochain.

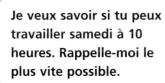

Messages telephoniques / Telephone messages

Allô.
Hello.

Bonjour. Je voudrais parler à Monsieur Grand s'il vous plaît.
Hello, I would like to speak to Mr Grand please.

Je regrette Monsieur Grand n'est pas ici.
I'm afraid Mr Grand isn't here.

Je peux laisser un message?
Can I leave a message?

Oui, c'est de la part de qui?
Yes, who should I say called?

C'est Jon Dupui à l'appareil. J'ai un téléphone portable, mon numéro est 86 73 45.
It is Jon Dupui speaking. I have a mobile telephone, my number is 86 73 45.

OK, je donnerai à Monsieur Grand votre numéro de téléphone.
OK, I will give Mr Grand your telephone number.

Merci beaucoup. Si je suis occupé, il peut laisser un message au répondeur et je vais rappeler plus tard.
Thank you. If I am busy, he can leave a message on the machine and I will call again later.

Au cinémá ou au théâtre / At the cinema or theatre

le cinéma	cinema
le théâtre	theatre
le cirque	a star
un acteur / une actrice	actor / actress
un chanteur / une chanteuse	singer
une chanson	a song
une pièce (de théâtre)	a play
un spectacle	a show
une séance	a performance
une salle	a screen
le balcon	circle
une place	a seat
l'entrée	entrance fee
un dessin animé	animated film
un film comique	comedy
un film d'amour	romantic film
un film d'aventures	adventure film
un film d'épouvante	scary film
un film d'horreur	horror film
un film policier	detective film
un film de science fiction	science fiction film
sous-titré	sub-titled
version française (VF)	French version
version originale (VO)	original version

Au bureau de billet / At the ticket office

Je voudrais trois places, pour un adulte et deux enfants.
I'd like 3 seats, for one adult and two children.
Est-ce qu'il y a des réductions pour les étudiants?
Are there reductions for students?
A quelle heure commence le film?
What time does the film start?
L'entrée, c'est combien?
How much is it to get in?

? Test Yourself!

In French, how would you...?

1. Ask if there are any reductions for children.
2. Book 4 seats, for 2 adults and 2 children.
3. Ask what time the film finishes.
4. Ask the price for one adult ticket

La télévision / Television

un documentaire	a documentary
les informations	news
la météo	weather forecast
la publicité	advertisement
une série	series
la télé-réalité	reality TV
un feuilleton	a soap
une émission	a programme

une émission musicale / sportive / pour enfants
a music / sports / children's programme

Task

What sort of programme would you recommend for the following?

1. **Annick aime les matches de football.**
2. **Bernadette préfère les concerts.**
3. **Cécile adore lire le journal.**
4. **Danielle aime les animaux sauvages.**

Leisure

Les invitations / Invitations

Tu veux aller...?	Do you want to go...?
... au cinéma ce soir?	... to the cinema tonight?
... au concert samedi?	... to the concert on Saturday?
... au théâtre demain?	... to the theatre tomorrow?
... au restaurant avec moi?	... to the restaurant with me?

On accepte / To accept

Je veux bien.	I'd love to.
Avec plaisir!	With pleasure!
Bonne idée.	Good idea.
Oui, d'accord.	Yes, OK.
Pourquoi pas?	Why not?

On refuse / To refuse

Non, merci.	No thank you.
Certainement pas!	Certainly not.
Je n'ai pas envie d'y aller.	I don't feel like going.
Désolé, je ne peux pas.	Sorry, I can't.
Fiche-moi la paix!	Get lost!

Des excuses / Excuses

Je dois me laver les cheveux.	I've got to wash my hair.
Je dois garder ma petite sœur.	I've got to look after my little sister.
Je dois aller chez mes grands-parents.	I've got to visit my grandparents.
Je dois finir mes devoirs.	I've got to finish my homework.

Les arrangements / Arrangements

On se retrouve à quelle heure?	What time should we meet?
On se retrouve où?	Where should we meet?
Chez moi / toi.	At my / your house.
Devant le cinéma / théâtre / stade.	In front of the cinema / theatre / stadium.
À l'arrêt d'autobus / à la gare routière.	At the bus stop / at the bus station.

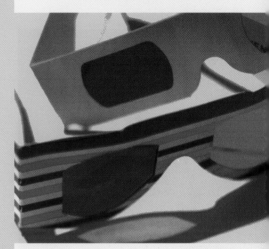

(?) Test Yourself!

Practise responding to these invitations:

1. **Tu veux aller au match de foot ce soir?**
2. **Tu veux aller au café avec moi?**
3. **Tu veux aller à la plage le week-end prochain?**
4. **Tu veux aller au cinéma demain?**
5. **Tu veux aller au musée samedi?**

Grammaire (Irregular Verbs)

The irregular verbs **devoir** (to have to / must), **vouloir** (to want), **pouvoir** (to be able / can), **savoir** (to know / know how to) are very useful. Here they are in full:

devoir	to have to (must)	savoir	to know (know how to)
je dois	I must	**je sais**	I know
tu dois	you must	**tu sais**	you know
il / elle / on doit	he/she/one must	**il / elle / on sait**	he/she/one knows
nous devons	we must	**nous savons**	we know
vous devez	you must	**vous savez**	you know
ils / elles doivent	they must	**ils / elles savent**	they know

pouvoir	to be able (can)	vouloir	to want
je peux	I can	**je veux**	I want
tu peux	you can	**tu veux**	you want
il / elle / on peut	he/she/one can	**il / elle / on veut**	he/she/one wants
nous pouvons	we can	**nous voulons**	we want
vous pouvez	you can	**vous voulez**	you want
ils / elles peuvent	they can	**ils / elles veulent**	they want

When you use these verbs they are always followed by the infinitive (see page 87). They can be used in many different contexts:

- **Tu veux aller au cinéma?**	Do you want to go to the cinema?
- **Oui, je veux bien.**	I'd like to.
- **Non, je ne veux pas.**	I don't want to.
- **Voulez-vous venir avec nous?**	Do you want to come with us?
- **Je ne peux pas aller au cinéma, parce que je dois faire du babysitting.**	I can't go to the cinema, because I have to babysit
- **Pouvez-vous m'aider?**	Can you help me?
- **Je ne sais pas.**	I don't know.

Note:

Je voudrais (I'd like to) comes from **vouloir**.
Je pourrais (I might/I could) comes from **pouvoir**.
Je devrais (I ought/I should) comes from **devoir**.

Make sure you understand the difference in meaning between these verbs:

Je ne peux pas conduire
I can't drive
(e.g. because I've broken my leg)
Je ne sais pas conduire
I can't drive
(e.g. I don't know how to)
Il ne peut pas nager
He can't swim
(e.g. because he's forgotten his costume)
Il ne sait pas nager
He can't swim
(e.g. he's never learned)

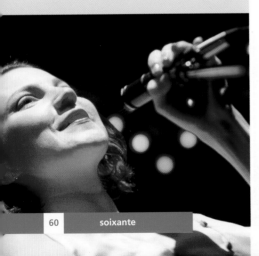

Leisure

Useful Phrases

J'adore le rap et le R et B. Mon chanteur préféré est Monsieur Bling parce qu'il est très beau. Je ne joue pas d'un instrument.
I love rap and R&B. My favourite singer is Mr Bling, because he is very good-looking. I don't play an instrument.

Je regarde la télé presque tous les jours. J'aime surtout les feuilletons. Je vais au cinéma de temps en temps. Mon acteur préféré est Brent Etoile.
I watch TV nearly every day. I especially like soaps. I occasionally go to the cinema. My favourite actor is Brent Etoile.

Je ne regarde pas très souvent la télé - je la trouve débile - mais je vais au cinéma une fois par semaine. Je préfère les films comiques.
I don't watch TV very often - I think it's stupid - but I go to the cinema once a week. I prefer comedies.

Je déteste le rap mais j'aime bien le jazz et la musique classique. Ma chanteuse préférée est Simone Lyrique parce qu'elle a beaucoup de talent. Je sais jouer du piano.
I hate rap, but I really like jazz and classical music. My favourite singer is Simone Lyrique because she is very talented. I can play the piano.

Préférences et opinions / Preferences and opinions

- **Je ne veux pas aller au concert parce que ça finit trop tard / c'est trop loin.**
  I don't want to go to the concert because it finishes too late / is too far away.
- **J'aimerais mieux aller au théâtre parce que ce sera intéressant.**
  I would rather go to the theatre because it will be interesting.
- **Je veux voir ce film au cinéma. Il s'agit de…**
  I want to see this film at the cinema. It's about…
- **Je vais au stade une fois par semaine. Mon équipe préférée est…**
  I go to the football ground once a week. My favourite team is…
- **Je suis allé au match samedi dernier. Mon équipe a bien joué, on a gagné.**
  I went to a match last Saturday. My team played well, we won.
- **Mon équipe n'a pas bien joué. On a perdu / C'était match nul.**
  My team didn't play well. We lost / It was a draw.

 Task

Write a short description of what your favourite film is about e.g. **il s'agit de…**

? Test Yourself!

Can you identify the following…?

1. **C'est une émission de télévision, un feuilleton. Il s'agit des habitants d'une rue dans le nord-ouest de l'Angleterre.**
2. **C'est un film, un dessin animé. Il s'agit des aventures d'une princesse, Blanche-Neige, qui habite dans une forêt avec sept petits hommes.**
3. **C'est une pièce de théâtre, une tragédie de William Shakespeare. Elle s'agit d'un jeune homme qui habite au Danemark et qui voit le fantôme de son père qui a été assassiné par son frère.**

Les magasins / Shops

la banque	bank
une bijouterie	jeweller
une boucherie	butcher
une boulangerie	baker
une boutique	shop
un centre commercial	shopping centre
une charcuterie	pork butcher
une confiserie	sweet shop
une épicerie	grocer
un grand magasin	department store
un hypermarché	hypermarket
une librairie	book shop
le marché	market
une parfumerie	perfume shop
une pâtisserie	cake shop
une pharmacie	chemist
un supermarché	supermarket
un bureau de tabac	tobacconist

Quantités / Quantities

une boîte	a tin / box
une bouteille	a bottle
un flacon	a small bottle (perfume)
un kilo	one kilo
un litre	one litre
un livre	half a kilo (500g)
un paquet	a packet
un pot	a jar
une tasse	a cup
un verre	a glass
une paire	a pair

Helpful Hint

It does not matter whether an item is masculine, feminine, singular or plural, when you ask for a quantity of something always use **de (d')**.

- **du fromage**	some cheese
une livre de fromage	500g of cheese
- **de la limonade**	some lemonade
une bouteille de limonade	a bottle of lemonade
- **de l'eau minérale**	some mineral water
un verre d'eau minérale	a glass of mineral water
- **des chocolats**	some chocolates
une boîte de chocolats	a box of chocolates

Shopping

Les vêtements/Clothes

un anorak	anorak
des baskets	trainers
un blouson	jacket
une casquette	cap
un chapeau	hat
des chaussettes	socks
des chaussures	shoes
une chemise	shirt
une cravate	tie
un imperméable	raincoat
un jean	jeans
une jupe	skirt
un manteau	coat
un maillot	bathing costume
une minijupe	miniskirt
un mouchoir	handkerchief
un pantalon	trousers
un pullover	jumper
un pyjama	pyjamas
une robe	dress
un sweat-shirt	sweatshirt
un short	shorts
un T-shirt	T-shirt
une veste	jacket
en coton	made of cotton
en cuir	made of leather
en laine	made of wool
en soie	made of silk

e.g. une chemise en coton
    a cotton shirt

Useful Phrases

Je voudrais...	I would like...
j'aimerais...	I would like...
avez-vous...?	have you...?
s'il vous plaît	please
merci	thank you
c'est combien?	how much?
ça fait combien?	how much is that?
c'est trop cher.	it's too dear.
ce n'est pas cher.	it's cheap.
avec ça?	anything else?
c'est tout, merci.	that's all, thanks.
Quelle taille?	What size?
Quelle pointure?	What size? (of shoes)
De quelle couleur?	What colour?
Je peux essayer...?	Can I try on...?

Où est la cabine d'essayage?
Where is the changing room?
Avez-vous la même chemise en bleu?
Have you the same shirt in blue?
Ça ne me va pas.
It doesn't suit me.
C'est trop grand / petit.
It's too big / small.
C'est trop long / court.
It's too long / short.
C'est trop large / étroit.
It's too baggy / tight.

? Test Yourself!

1 Which shop would you visit to buy...?
    ...une montre (a watch)
    ...le parfum (perfume)
    ...l'alimentation (groceries)
    ...un parapluie (umbrella)

2 How would you ask for...?
    ...a litre of red wine
    ...a jar of jam
    ...a packet of tea
    ...a tin of tomatoes

3 What would you wear to...?
    ...a wedding
    ...a birthday party
    ...the cinema
    ...school

NB adjectives have to agree with the nouns e.g. **une chemise bleue, une veste courte, des chaussures noires**.

Plaintes / Complaints

Je voudrais me plaindre....
I'd like to complain...
J'ai acheté cette chemise
hier / jeudi dernier
I bought this shirt yesterday
/ last Thursday
Il y a un trou dedans
It has a hole in it
C'est déchiré
It's torn
J'ai acheté cet appareil-photo ici
I bought this camera here
Il ne marche pas
It doesn't work
Vous pouvez me le rembourser?
Can I have my money back?
Voici le reçu
Here's the receipt
Je voudrais voir le directeur
I'd like to see the manager
Ce n'est pas la bonne
taille / couleur
It's not the right size / colour

Signes de magasin / Shop signs

une offre (spéciale)
(special) offer
soldes
sale
rabais / réductions
discount
Si vous en achetez un, vous
en aurez un autre gratuit!
Buy one get one free!
moins 20%
20% off
ouvert
open
fermé
closed
heures d'ouverture
opening times
congé annuel
annual closing
Ouvert tous les jours, sauf...
Open daily, except...

Keywords

les achats	purchases	**un sac à main**	handbag
acheter	to buy	**le sous-sol**	basement
la caisse	cash desk	**le rez-de-chaussée**	ground floor
une carte de crédit	credit card	**un étage**	floor
un portefeuille	wallet	**un rayon**	department
un porte-monnaie	purse	**un marchand**	shopkeeper
dépenser	to spend	**un ascenseur**	lift / elevator

Grammaire (Demonstrative Adjectives)

You need to know how to say *this, that, these* and *those*.

	Ce pullover	*this* jumper (masculine)
	Cette veste	*this* jacket (feminine)
	Ces chaussures	*these* shoes (plural)
but	**cet anorak**	*this* anorak (masculine but starts with a vowel)

If you want to be absolutely clear, add **-ci** or **-là** to the word.
ce pullover-ci is *this* jumper but **ce pullover-là** is *that* jumper
ces chaussettes-ci is *these* socks but **ces chaussettes-là** is *those* socks

Shopping

Useful Phrases

- Pendant ma visite j'ai acheté...
- Je cherchais..., j'ai trouvé...
- Je ne pouvais pas résister...
- J'avais faim donc...
- J'ai décidé de...
- J'ai essayé...
- Mon père adore..., donc c'était parfait pour lui.
- Je pense que le cadeau est parfait pour elle.
- Je ne veux pas retourner, parce que...
- Je vais certainement retourner.
- La prochaine fois...
- J'ai l'intention de passer plus longtemps...
- Je ne veux pas dépenser trop d'argent.
- J'irai seul(e) / j'irai avec...

- During my visit I bought...
- I was looking for..., I found...
- I couldn't resist...
- I was hungry so...
- I decided to...
- I tried on...
- My dad loves..., so it was perfect for him.
- I think this present is perfect for her.
- I don't want to go back because...
- I will definitely go back.
- Next time...
- I intend to spend longer...

- I don't want to spend too much money.
- I'll go alone / I'll go with...

Le centre commercial / The shopping centre

Le weekend dernier, je suis allée à un centre commercial qui s'appelle Champs Verts. J'y suis allée avec ma soeur. Je voulais faire du shopping parce qu'il me fallait trouver un cadeau pour l'anniversaire de mon père.
Last weekend I went to a shopping centre called Green Fields. I went there with my sister. I wanted to go shopping because I wanted to find a birthday present for my father.

Samedi, j'ai passé la journée au centre commercial qui se trouve à Salford près de Manchester. J'ai dû visiter le centre commercial parce que j'avais besoin de nouveaux vêtements.
On Saturday I spent the day at a shopping centre which is situated in Salford near Manchester. I had to visit the centre because I needed new clothes.

Le centre est un grand bâtiment moderne au centre de Londres. Dans le centre il y a beaucoup de magasins de toutes sortes, mais il y a trop de monde.
The centre is a large modern building in the centre of London. In the centre, there are lots of shops of all kinds, but there are too many people.

Il y a un bon choix de magasins dans le centre. Il y a en plus un cinéma et beaucoup de restaurants. On peut manger la cuisine américaine, indienne, chinoise, italienne... Cependant, il est difficile de garer la voiture.
There is a good choice of shops at the centre. What's more there is a cinema and lots of restaurants. One can eat American food, Indian food, Chinese food, Italian food... However, it is hard to park the car.

 Task

Write an account of a visit to a shopping centre, try to make it as varied and interesting as possible.

Les rapports / Relationships

J'aime bien mon petit ami, Marc...
I like my boyfriend, Marc, a lot...

J'aime mon épouse...
I love my wife...

J'adore mon meilleur ami...
I adore my best friend...

Je m'entends bien avec ma mère...
I get on well with my mother...

Je ne m'entends pas du tout avec mon frère...
I don't get on with my brother...

parce qu'il est...	because he is...
parce qu'elle est...	because she is...
sympa	nice
casse-pieds	a nuisance
gentil(le)	kind
impatient(e)	impatient
généreux / généreuse	generous
impoli(e)	impolite
amusant(e)	funny
méchant(e)	nasty
drôle	witty
paresseux / paresseuse	lazy
patient(e)	patient
timide	shy
poli(e)	polite
egoïste	selfish
sportif / sportive	sporty
sévère	strict
intelligent(e)	clever
ennuyeux / ennuyeuse	boring
pleine de vie	full of life
sérieux / sérieuse	serious
sage	well-behaved
bête	stupid
honnête	honest
bavard(e)	gossipy
gai(e)	cheerful
jaloux / jalouse	jealous
aimable	friendly
maladroit(e)	clumsy

Keywords

aimer bien	to like a lot	**une petite amie**	girlfriend
aimer mieux	to prefer	**la permission**	permission
critiquer	to criticise	**faire la connaissance**	to get to know
se disputer	to argue	**se rencontrer**	to meet
s'entendre avec	to get on with	**des rapports**	relationships
épouser	to marry	**un sens de l'humeur**	sense of humour
l'amour	love	**une dispute**	an argument
un petit ami	boyfriend		

(?) Test Yourself!

From the information given, which word (or quality) do you think best describes each of the family members below?

e.g. **Mon père joue au tennis, il fait du jogging et il aime le foot.**
Il est sportif.
Ma sœur a toujours de bonne notes à l'école. Elle est intelligente.

1. **Mon frère ne travaille pas à la maison et il ne fait jamais ses devoirs.**
2. **Ma mère me donne beaucoup d'argent de poche et elle achète des vêtements pour moi.**
3. **Mon père est très strict et il ne me permet pas de sortir avec mes amis.**
4. **Mon demi-frère n'est pas drôle et il n'aime pas sortir.**
5. **Ma demi-sœur est sympa, elle m'écoute quand j'ai des problèmes.**

onal Relationships

Useful Phrases

- **Nous avons les mêmes intérêts.**
- **Nous n'avons rien en commun.**
- **Je peux lui parler quand
  j'ai un problème.**
- **Ils ne me comprennent pas.**
- **Nous ne nous disputons jamais.**
- **Nous nous disputons tout le temps.**
- **Ils critiquent mon travail /
  mes opinions.**

- We have the same interests.
- We don't have anything in common.
- I can talk to him/her when
  I have a problem.
- They don't understand me.
- We never argue.
- We argue all the time.
- They criticise my work/opinions.

Helpful Hint

Intensifiers can be very useful when you are describing someone's character and personality.

très	very
trop	too
assez	fairly/quite
un peu	a little bit
beaucoup	a lot

e.g. **Il est trop sérieux**
   He's too serious
   Elle est assez timide
   She's fairly (quite) shy

Marie-Pierre

Ma meilleure amie est gentille et généreuse. Elle a le même âge que moi et elle est intelligente et très drôle, mais quelquefois elle est un peu paresseuse. Elle aime bien les chevaux et elle déteste les champignons. Je peux lui parler de tout.

My best friend is kind and generous. She is the same age as me and she is clever and very witty, but sometimes she can be a bit lazy. She really likes horses and she hates mushrooms. I can talk to her about anything.

Chantal

Mon partenaire idéal est grand et beau. Il est plus âgé que moi. Il est honnête, gentil et poli, amusant et intelligent. Il n'est pas trop sérieux ou ennuyeux. Il est plein de vie. Il aime le cinéma et le théâtre et il n'aime pas le foot!

My ideal partner is tall and handsome. He is older than me. He is honest, kind and polite, funny and intelligent. He isn't too serious or boring. He is full of life. He likes the cinema and theatre and he doesn't like football!

Character and Pe

Les disputes / Arguments

Je me dispute avec ma soeur à cause de mes vêtements. Elle emprunte toujours mes affaires.
I argue with my sister about my clothes. She is always borrowing my things.

Je me dispute avec mes parents à cause des sorties. Je dois toujours rentrer à dix heures. Ce n'est pas juste!
I argue with my parents about going out. I always have to be home by 10. It's not fair!

Je me dispute avec mon frère à cause de la musique. Nous n'avons pas les mêmes goûts.
I argue with my brother about music. We have different tastes.

 Task

Here are four subjects that you might disagree with your parents on. Form two sentences for each example, matching the subject to one of the reasons given below.

e.g. **Je me dispute avec mes parents à cause de mes vêtements.** Ils pensent que les slogans sur mes t-shirts sont offensants.

1 **de mes études.**
2 **de l'argent.**
3 **de ma chambre.**
4 **du ménage.**

A **Mes amis reçoivent plus d'argent de poche que moi.**
B **Je dois finir mes corvées avant de sortir.**
C **Ils pensent pas que je ne travaille pas assez.**
D **Ils disent que c'est en désordre.**

Grammaire (Comparative and Superlative)

If you want to compare two people, there are three very useful words: **plus** (more), **moins** (less) and **aussi** (also).

e.g. **Mon frère est** plus **sportif que ma sœur.**
My brother is sportier (more sporty) than my sister.
Mon grand-père est moins **sévère que mes parents.**
My grandfather is less strict than my parents.
Ma sœur est aussi **intelligente que moi.**
My sister is as clever as I am.

To say the most, you use **le plus** or **la plus** to agree with the subject.

e.g. **Mon ami est l'élève** le plus **intelligent de la classe.**
My friend is the most intelligent pupil in the class.
Ma sœur est la personne la plus **égoïste du monde.**
My sister is the most selfish person in the world.

The French word for better is **meilleur.** With a verb, you use **mieux.**

e.g. **Mon ami est un** meilleur **chanteur que moi.**
My friend is a better singer than me (singer is a noun).
Mon ami chante mieux **que moi.**
My friend sings better than me (sing is a verb).

To say the best, use **le meilleur**, **la meilleure** or **les meilleur(e)s:**

e.g. **Accrington Stanley est** la meilleure **équipe de foot**.
Accrington Stanley is the best football team.

onal Relationships

YOUR SHOUT
letters

Annie, 15 ans.

Mon problème? Je déteste aller à l'école. Les professeurs ne s'intéressent pas aux élèves. Je trouve mes cours très difficiles. Je n'ai pas d'amis. La semaine dernière, j'ai rencontré un garçon très sympa, mais je suis trop timide et je ne peux pas lui parler.

Marie, 14 ans.

Chez moi, il est très difficile en ce moment. Je n'ai pas de frères ni de sœurs et mes parents ne me permettent pas de sortir avec mes amis. Ils me critiquent tout le temps et me disent que je dois rester à la maison pour faire mon travail scolaire.

All letters printed receive a suprise gift box.

Paul, 15 ans.

Je ne peux pas parler à mes parents parce qu'ils ne me comprennent pas, mais j'ai un gros problème au collège. Il y a un garçon dans ma classe qui me dit des choses désagréables et il a menacé de me battre. J'ai peur de lui. Que dois-je faire?

 Exam Practice

Read the problem page letters opposite and answer the questions:

1. Who hates school?
2. Name one of the reasons why.
3. Who is an only child?
4. Why are they not allowed to go out?
5. Who is being bullied at school?
6. Why can't they tell their parents?

 Task

Who is your favourite celebrity? Write a short description of them, including all the personality traits and qualities that make you like them.

Test Yourself!

1. In French, how do you say…?
   …my French teacher is funnier than my maths teacher.
   …my aunty is less hard-working than my mother.
   …I am as witty as my brother.

2. Name the following people/things, according to your personal opinion.
   …L'acteur le plus beau du monde (ou l'actrice la plus belle du monde).
   …Le meilleur chanteur (ou la meilleure chanteuse).
   …La ville la plus jolie du monde.
   …Le film le plus amusant.
   …L'émission de télé la plus intéressante.

Keywords

un logement	accommodation / housing	la Terre	the Earth
la cité	housing estate	le monde	the world
les H.L.M.	low cost / public sector housing	un centre de recyclage	recycling centre
(habitation à loyer modéré)		les déchets	waste
une maison individuelle	detached house	l'environnement	the environment
une maison jumelée	semi-detached	l'espace vert	green belt
une maison mitoyenne	terraced house	la fumée	smoke
un studio	bed-sit	jeter	to throw away
la circulation	traffic	les papiers	litter (papers)
un camion	lorry	par terre	on the ground
un embouteillage	traffic jam	le pétrole	oil / petrol
les heures d'affluence	rush hour	pollué	polluted
les transports en commun	public transport	la pollution	pollution
une zone piétonne	pedestrian zone	le trottoir	pavement
		le gaz	gas

? Test Yourself!

From the list of keywords, choose the one that best matches each of these definitions.

1. C'est un endroit où l'on peut recycler le verre, le papier etc.
2. Les trains, les autobus et les tramways.
3. En ville, c'est un endroit où les voitures ne sont pas permises.
4. C'est quand tout le monde va au travail ou rentre à la maison en fin de journée.
5. C'est notre planète.
6. C'est un véhicule qui transporte des marchandises.
7. C'est un endroit où il y a des arbres, des fleurs et des pelouses et il n'y a pas beaucoup de bâtiments.

Exam Practice

1. Who lives in the country?
2. Who lives in a town centre?
3. Who has the smallest accommodation?
4. Who lives in a large house?
5. Who doesn't like the area in which he/she lives?

C Moi, j'habite dans un appartement au centre-ville. J'aime bien habiter ici, c'est très pratique. Il y a deux chambres et un salon.

B J'habite une maison individuelle dans la banlieue d'une grande ville. Il y a cinq chambres et deux salles de bains. Nous avons aussi deux jardins.

A Je suis étudiant et j'habite un petit studio près de l'université. Il n'y a pas beaucoup d'espace mais ça ne coûte pas très cher.

D Moi, j'habite une cité d'H.L.M. au nord de Paris. Nous avons trois chambres. Mon quartier n'est pas agréable - il y a beaucoup de graffiti et des papiers par terre.

E J'habite une ferme à la campagne. C'est très calme et tranquille.

The Environment

Les problèmes / The problems

A mon avis, le problème le plus grave, c'est la pollution.
In my opinion, the most serious problem is pollution.
Je m'inquiète du réchauffement de la terre et de l'effet de serre.
I am worried about global warming and the greenhouse effect.
Certaines espèces d'animaux deviennent très rares.
Some species of animals are becoming extinct.
La pluie acide détruit l'environnement.
Acid rain is destroying the environment.
Bientôt, il n'y aura plus de combustibles fossiles.
Soon there will not be any fossil fuels left.

Les raisons / The causes

Les usines polluent l'atmosphère.
Factories are polluting the atmosphere.
Les aérosols produisent des CFCs.
Aerosols give off CFCs.
Les magasins et les fabricants utilisent trop d'emballage.
Shops and manufacturers use too much packaging.
On ne recycle pas assez de déchets.
We do not recycle enough waste.
On détruit des forêts pour construire plus de maisons.
We are cutting down forests to build more houses.

Qu'est-ce qu'on peut faire? / What can we do?

Il faut utiliser l'énergie éolienne et solaire.
We should use wind power and solar power.
On peut recycler le papier, le métal et le plastique.
We can recycle paper, metal and plastic.
Il faut protéger les animaux sauvages.
We need to protect wild animals.
Il faut conserver les ressources naturelles / l'énergie.
We must conserve natural resources / energy.

Task

Here are six ways in which we can help to sustain natural resources. The sentences below describe easy ways in which individuals can contribute. Organise the methods and descriptions into matching pairs.

1. Saving electricity
2. Saving water
3. Recycling paper
4. Cutting down on packaging
5. Avoiding using the central heating
6. Recycling glass

A **Quand il fait froid en hiver, je mets un pullover au lieu d'utiliser le chauffage central.**
B **J'éteins toujours la lumière quand je quitte une pièce.**
C **Aujourd'hui, en France, seule une bouteille sur trois est recyclée. C'est une honte.**
D **Je recycle les journaux. Cela permet de sauver des forêts.**
E **Je ferme le robinet quand je me brosse les dents et je me douche au lieu de prendre un bain.**
F **J'achète toujours des biscuits emballés dans du carton, plutôt que dans du plastique.**

Points De Vue

Les Problèmes

'Il y a trop de poids lourds et voitures sur la route et les problèmes de circulation sont pires aux heures de pointe. Si plus de gens utilisaient les transports publics, il y aurait moins de voitures sur les routes. Je vais au collège à pied. C'est mieux pour l'environnement.'

There are too many lorries on the road and the congestion is worse at rush hour. If more people used public transport, there would be fewer cars on the road. I walk to school. It is better for the environment.

'J'ai une voiture. Les transports publics dans la ville sont très efficaces, mais à la campagne, il y à très peu de trains ni de bus. Ils sont sales et inefficaces aussi.'

I have a car. The public transport system in the city is very good, but in the country there are hardly any trains and buses. They are dirty and unreliable too.

Grammaire (The Conditional Tense)

The *conditional* tense is a form of future tense, which allows you to say what you *would* do. It is conditional because it refers to things that you *would* do if circumstances allowed (i.e. if certain *conditions* were met).

e.g. **Si je gagnais à la loterie nationale, j'achèterais une grosse voiture de sport**
If I won the lottery, I would buy a large sports car.

To form the conditional tense, use exactly the same stem as the future tense (see page 48) and add the following endings:

Je visiterais	I would visit	**Nous aur**ions	We would have
Tu serais	You would be	**Vous finir**iez	You would finish
Il achèterait	He would buy	**Ils ir**aient	They would go
Elle travaillerait	She would work	**Elles manger**aient	They would eat

The conditional is often used with the imperfect tense:

e.g. **Si** j'étais **riche, j'achèter**ais **une grande maison.**
If I was rich, I would buy a big house.
Si c'était **possible, je recycler**ais **le papier.**
If it was possible, I would recycle paper.

Make sure you learn these useful conditional phases:

Je voudrais...	I would like...
On devrait...	One ought...
On pourrait...	One might / could...

The Environment

1. How many differences can you find in the two descriptions?
2. Using these descriptions make lists of all the advantages and disadvantages of living
   a) in the country, and b) in a town.

Laurent

Limoges se trouve dans le centre de la France. C'est une grande ville industrielle. Il y a un centre commercial, un centre sportif, un théâtre, une cathédrale, et un musée.

Je n'aime pas habiter à Limoges parce qu'il n'y a rien à faire et c'est très ennuyeux. Ma ville est sale et polluée. Il y a des papiers et des graffiti partout.

Je préfère la campagne parce que c'est beau, tranquille et calme. En ville l'air est pollué. A la campagne on peut faire des promenades et respirer l'air pur.

Patricia

Caen se trouve dans le nord-ouest de la France près de Rouen. C'est une grande ville industrielle. Il y a un centre commercial, un centre sportif, une piscine, un stade, un théâtre, un cinéma, un musée et une bibliothèque. On peut faire du sport, faire des promenades à la campagne, faire du shopping.

J'aime bien habiter à Caen parce qu'il y a beaucoup à faire et c'est très animé. En ville on peut faire du shopping, il y a toujours quelque chose à faire.

Je n'aime pas la campagne. Je préfère la ville parce que la campagne est trop tranquille, il n'y a rien à faire. Il n'y a pas de transport.

A l'avenir je voudrais habiter dans un grand appartement à New York, parce que j'adore faire du shopping.

Test Yourself!

1. In French, describe your local environment and say what could be done to improve it. Use these phrases to help get started:

   Ma ville est / n'est pas....
   My town is / isn't...
   Il y a trop de (d')...
   There's too much / too many...
   Il n'y a pas assez de (d')...
   There are not enough...
   On devrait / pourrait…
   One ought to / could…

2. Translate the phrases below into French to complete the following sentence:

   Si j'étais un député…
   If I was a Member of Parliament...
   …I would create a pedestrian zone in the town centre.
   …I would improve public transport.
   …I would provide more recycling centres.

3. Now come up with two more things you would do to help improve the local environment if you were an MP.

Helpful Hint

You will find the following verbs useful when it comes to talking about ways of improving the environment, locally and globally.

nettoyer	to clean
créer	to create
réduire	to reduce
diminuer	to reduce
protéger	to protect
développer	to develop
supprimer	to get rid of
améliorer	to improve
construire	to build
augmenter	to increase
conserver	to conserve/save
fournir	to provide
utiliser	to use/make use of

L'enseignement/Education

une école maternelle	nursery
une école primaire	primary school
un collège	secondary school (ages 11-15)
un lycée	upper secondary school (ages 15-18)
un lycée technique	vocational sixth-form college
une école publique/privée	a public (state)/private school
un(e) pensionnaire	a boarder
un(e) demi-pensionnaire	a half-boarder (stays for lunch)
le brevet	exam taken at the end of le collège
le bac(calauréat)	French equivalent of A levels
le redoublement	repeating a year if not enough progress has been mad
le conseil de classe	meeting of teachers where pupils' progress is discusse

Les avis/Opinions

Il est important de faire des études si on veut un emploi bien payé.
It is important to get a good education if you want a well-paid job.
Même si on travaille dur, on n'obtient pas toujours un bon emploi.
Even if you work hard, you don't always get a good job.
J'aime aller à l'école pour voir tous mes amis.
I like going to school because I can see all my friends.
L'école est une préparation pour la vie active.
School prepares you for working life.
J'aime apprendre des choses nouvelles.
I enjoy learning new things.
Je déteste être enfermé(e) toute la journée.
I hate being stuck indoors all day.

Le règlement/Rules

il faut/il ne faut pas
you must (it is necessary)/you must not (it is not necessary)
on peut/on ne peut pas
you can/you cannot
on doit/on ne doit pas
you must/you must not
il est interdit de
it is forbidden to
il n'est pas permis de
It is not permitted to

Keywords

attaquer	to attack
causer	to chat
encourager	to encourage
garder	to keep/look after
protéger	to protect
sécher un cours	to truant
les affaires de sport	sports things (kit)
à la mode	fashionable
la bijouterie	jewellery
chic	smart
démodé	old-fashioned
le maquillage	make-up
la discipline	discipline
des graffiti	graffiti
la protection	protection
la sécurité	safety
le vandalisme	vandalism
la violence	violence
une note	a mark/grade
une option	an option
une règle	a rule
un résultat	a result
une retenue	a detention
apprenti(e)	apprentice
la formation continue	in-service training
la formation professionnelle	vocational training

Education

Helpful Hint

You can develop short, basic sentences, using the following words to introduce additional information and make what you say/write more interesting.

mais	but
et	and
donc	so/therefore
car	since/for
à cause de	because of
parce que	because
malgré	in spite of

Je vais étudier la biologie, parce que je veux être vétérinaire.
I'm going to study biology, *because* I want to be a vet.

Je veux être chef, mais il est difficile de trouver un restaurant qui accepte les stagiaires.
I want to be a chef, *but* it's hard to find a restaurant that accepts trainees.

Elle a obtenu un bon emploi malgré ses mauvaises notes.
She got a good job *despite* her poor grades.

J'ai l'intention de devenir médecin, donc je dois aller à l'université.
I intend to become a doctor, *so* I must go to university.

De bonnes notes sont importantes car il y a tant de demandeurs d'emploi.
Good grades are important *since* there are so many people seeking jobs.

On lui a offert le poste à cause de la formation qu'il a reçue.
He was offered the job *because of* the training he had received.

Grammaire (Ongoing and Recent Actions)

In French, to talk about actions that are still taking place you need to use the present tense.

- **Je fais de l'anglais depuis trois ans.** — I've been doing English for three years.
- **J'étudie l'espagnol depuis deux ans.** — I've been studying Spanish for two years.
- **J'apprends l'informatique depuis quatre ans.** — I've been learning IT for four years.
- **Je joue du violon depuis un an.** — I've been playing the violin for a year.

To describe actions that have just taken place and are now complete, the special expression **venir de** is used.

- **Je viens de quitter l'école.** — I've just left school.
- **Tu viens de commencer les études universitaires?** — Have you just started university?
- **Il vient de finir son apprentissage.** — He's just finished an apprenticeship.
- **Nous venons de passer les examens.** — We've just done our exams.
- **Vous venez de rentrer du travail?** — Have you just got back from work?
- **Elles viennent de finir leurs études.** — They have just finished their studies.

Task

1. Read this list of rules. Which ones are unlikely to be real school rules?
   - **Il faut manger en classe.**
   - **Il est interdit de fumer dans les toilettes.**
   - **On ne peut pas jouer au football à la cantine.**
   - **On doit laisser tomber des papiers.**
   - **Il n'est pas permis d'écrire des graffiti aux murs.**
   - **Il faut être insolent envers les professeurs.**
   - **Il est interdit de faire les devoirs.**

2. Use appropriate expressions to complete the following rules:
   ...être poli.
   ...boire de l'alcool au collège.
   ...sortir de l'école sans permission.
   ...être violent envers les autres.
   ...porter l'uniforme correct.

L'uniforme scolaire/School uniform

Je crois que l'uniforme scolaire est une très bonne idée parce qu'il n'est pas nécessaire de passer trop de temps à décider ce qu'il faut mettre pour aller au collège. On ne remarque plus les différences entre les riches et les pauvres non plus. Certains élèves dans ma classe arrivent tout le temps à l'école avec les nouveaux vêtements et les nouveaux baskets très chers.

I believe that school uniform is a very good idea, because you don't need to spend too much time deciding what to put on for school. You don't notice the differences between the rich and poor either. Some pupils in my class come to school with new clothes and very expensive new trainers all the time.

Moi, je suis contre l'uniforme scolaire. Il faut garder et protéger la liberté de l'individu. C'est triste quand tout le monde s'habille de la même manière. Notre uniforme est très démodé. On ne peut pas porter de bijoux ni de maquillage non plus.

I am against school uniform. It's necessary to look after and protect the freedom of the individual. It's sad when everyone dresses the same way. Our uniform is very old fashioned. We are not allowed to wear jewellery or make-up either.

Les Problèmes/Problems

Les activités extra-scolaires sont bien mais je n'ai pas le temps!
Extra-curricular activities are fine, but there's just no time!

Je n'ai pas de temps pour faire mes devoirs.
I don't have the time to do all my homework.

Le livre que je veux n'est jamais dans la bibliothèque.
The book I want is never in the library.

Il est difficile de travailler dans une salle de classe bruyante.
It is hard to work in a noisy classroom.

J'ai trois heures de devoirs tous les soirs. Je n'ai pas le temps de m'amuser!
I have 3 hours of homework each night. There is no time to have fun!

J'ai de bonnes notes, mais je vois rarement mes amis.
I get good grades, but I hardly ever see my friends.

Je trouve les maths difficiles, mais je ne suis pas bête.
I find maths hard, but I am not stupid.

Je ne comprends pas la physique. Les explications du prof ne sont pas bonnes.
I don't understand physics. The teacher does not explain it well.

? Test Yourself!

In French, how do you say...?
1. I like ICT a lot, so I am going to be an IT worker.
2. I'm going to study the sciences, because I want to be a doctor.
3. I want to be a teacher because of the long holidays.
4. I would like to be a policeman despite the uniform.
5. I am not going to university, since I hate school.
6. I've been studying French for 5 years.
7. I've been playing the piano for 6 years.
8. I've just done my exams.
9. I've just finished my studies and I've just started work.

Task

In French, write a...
1. ...short letter to the editor of a school newspaper explaining why you agree or disagree with school uniform.
2. ...description of **L'école idéale** (the ideal school). Include information about the facilities and what the teachers and pupils are like. Remember, you can use the negative to write about things that are absent e.g. vandalism and violence.

Education

These three teenagers are talking about their schools.

1 Who thinks the teachers are bad at their job?
2 What reason do they give for this?
3 Who thinks that pupils work too much?
4 What reason do they give for this?
5 Who complains about other pupils' bad behaviour?
6 Why do they think it is important to go to school and take exams?

Salma

L'école est très importante parce qu'il faut réussir à ses examens pour avoir un bon emploi. Mais il est souvent très difficile de travailler bien en classe parce que beaucoup d'élèves ne s'intéressent pas aux cours et ils n'écoutent pas le prof. Ils passent tout le temps à parler et cela est très énervant pour moi.

Abdul

Je déteste l'ambiance dans mon collège. C'est très stressant. Pour les profs, seulement les bonnes notes et les devoirs sont importants. On travaille trop tout le temps et on n' a pas assez de temps pour faire des loisirs. Je ne peux pas sortir le week-end parce qu'on a trop à faire.

Mélanie

A mon école, les professeurs ne sont pas très gentils. Ils ne s'intéressent pas aux élèves et ils ne nous écoutent pas. Je ne m'entends pas très bien avec eux. C'est triste.

Grammaire (Emphatic Pronouns)

In French, the *emphatic pronouns* can be used to stress or emphasise who you are talking about.

moi	me	**toi**	you
lui	him	**elle**	her
nous	us	**vous**	you
eux	them (m)	**elles**	them (f)

e.g. **Moi, j'aime les sciences, mais toi tu préfères l'anglais.**
Me, I like science, but you, you prefer English.
Il est très bête, lui.
He's very stupid, he is.

They are also used after prepositions such as **pour** (for), **avec** (with) and **sans** (without).

e.g. **L'allemand est très difficile pour moi.**
German is very difficult for me.
Je vais à l'école avec eux.
I go to school with them.

? Test Yourself!

Read the following statements and answer the questions below.

A **Moi, je vais au lycée technique et je fais une formation professionnelle, parce que je voudrais devenir mécanicien à la fin de mes études.**

B **Je vais au collège depuis deux ans. Ma matière préférée est l'anglais. Je l'aime beaucoup et c'est une matière très utile parce que je veux travailler à l'étranger plus tard dans la vie.**

C **Moi, je suis élève dans un lycée classique. J'étudie le latin et le grec, parce que je rêve d'aller à l'université et de devenir archéologue.**

1 What type of school does each of these students attend?
2 What are they studying and why?

Grammaire (L'avenir/The future)

There are two methods of expressing future plans. Spoken French tends to favour the use of **aller** + the infinitive (see page 24). Similarly, you can use the infinitive with the following phrases:

Je veux...	I want...	**Je voudrais...**	I would like...
J'espère...	I hope...	**J'ai l'intention de...**	I intend...
Je rêve de...	I dream of...		

e.g. **Je veux aller à l'université.** — I want to go to university.
Je vais étudier les sciences. — I'm going to study science.
Je voudrais voyager autour du monde. — I'd like to travel around the world.
J'espère devenir infirmière. — I hope to become a nurse.
J'ai l'intention de visiter les Etats-Unis. — I intend to visit the USA.
Je rêve de travailler en France. — I dream of working in France.

In written French it is more appropriate to use the future tense, formed by adding the correct ending to the infinitive (see page 48). The ending **-ai** is used with **je** (I).

Je visiterai...	I'll travel...	**Je voyagerai...**	I'll visit...
J'habiterai...	I'll live...	**Je travaillerai...**	I'll work...

e.g. **Je travaillerai dans une banque.** — I'll work in a bank.
Je visiterai Paris. — I'll visit Paris.

Exceptions that you will need to learn individually include...

J'aurai...	I will have...	**Je serai...**	I will be...
J'irai...	I will go...	**Je ferai...**	I'll do...

e.g. **Je serai riche et célèbre.** — I'll be rich and famous.
J'aurai deux enfants. — I'll have 2 children.

Note that **ce sera** is *it will be* e.g. **ce sera intéressant.**

Helpful Hint

When talking about career ambitions you will find the following phrases invaluable:

Je voudrais devenir... — I'd like to become...

You can then use **parce que/qu'** (because) or **malgré le fait que/qui** (in spite of the fact that) to give more information about your choice. Here are a few examples of what you might say:

... **il est très stressant.**	... it is very stressful.
... **il n'est pas valorisé.**	... it is not well regarded.
... **c'est bien payé/mal payé.**	... it's well paid/badly paid.
... **il faut travailler de longues heures.**	... you have to work long hours.
... **il faut travailler dans des conditions difficiles.**	... you have to work in difficult conditions.
... **il y a des possibilités pour l'avancement.**	... there are opportunities for promotion.
... **l'avancement est difficile.**	... it's hard to get promotion.

Mariage? Enfants?/Marriage? Children?

Je ne vais pas me marier. Il y a trop de divorces.
I am not going to get married. There are too many divorces.

Me marier et avoir des enfants, ça ne m'intéresse pas.
Marriage and having children do not interest me.

J'espère me marier avec mon homme idéal/ma femme idéale.
I hope to marry my ideal man/my ideal woman.

Je veux me marier à l'âge de...ans.
I want to marry at the age of...

Je voudrais deux/trois enfants.
I'd like two/three children.

Je rêve d'habiter dans une grande maison avec un jardin à la campagne.
I dream of living in a big house with a garden in the countryside.

Je veux une famille nombreuse.
I want to have a big family.

Je ne veux pas d'enfants.
I don't want children.

J'aurai des enfants, mais quand je serai plus âgé(e).
I will have children, but when I am older.

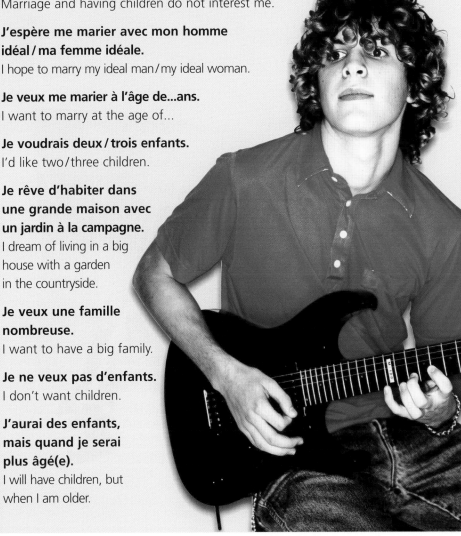

La pression/Pressure

Mes parents pensent que je devrais devenir chirurgien, mais je n'aime pas le sang.
My parents think I should be a surgeon, but I do not like blood.

Je veux devenir musicien, mais mes parents pensent que ce n'est pas une carrière souhaitable.
I want to be a musician, but my parents do not think it is a suitable career.

Mon père est avocat et il pense que je devrais faire le même travail que lui.
My father is a lawyer and he thinks I should do the same job as him.

Je voudrais entrer dans l'armée, mais ma mère serait bouleversée.
I want to join the army, but it would upset my mother.

Je ne sais pas ce que je veux faire. Je suis trop jeune pour faire des décisions comme ça.
I don't know what I want to do. I am too young to be making decisions like that.

Mon professeur de maths pense que je devrais être comptable, mais ça serait ennuyeux.
My maths teacher thinks I should be an accountant, but that would be boring.

 Task

Complete the sentences below, choosing an appropriate reason from those provided.

1. Je voudrais devenir fermier...
2. Je veux continuer mes études et je vais étudier les maths...
3. Je voudrais travailler comme comptable...
4. Je vais devenir professeur...
5. Je visiterai l'Espagne...
6. Je voudrais devenir hôtesse de l'air...
7. Je rêve d'habiter à la campagne dans une grande maison...
8. Je voudrais devenir médecin...

A. ...parce que j'adore les enfants.
B. ...parce que je suis fort en maths.
C. ...parce que ce sera calme et tranquille.
D. ...parce que c'est un travail bien payé.
E. ...parce que j'aime le climat chaud.
F. ...parce que je veux travailler en plein air.
G. ...parce que je veux guérir les malades.
H. ...parce que je veux voyager.

Useful Phrases

dans cinq ans	in five years' time
peut-être	perhaps
l'année prochaine	next year
probablement	probably
à l'âge de 21 ans	at the age of 21
si tout va bien	if all goes well
avant l'âge de...	before the age of...
à l'avenir	in the future
quand j'aurai 30 ans	when I'm 30
bientôt	soon
certainement	certainly

Les ambitions / Ambitions

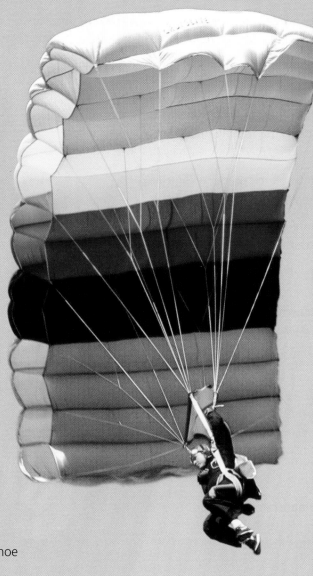

se marier	to marry
avoir des enfants	to have children
habiter à l'étranger	to live abroad
devenir riche et célèbre	to become rich and famous
rencontrer...	to meet...
nager avec les dauphins	to swim with dolphins
acheter une grande voiture	to buy a big car
conduire une moto	to drive a motorbike
faire du parachutisme	to go parachuting
faire un safari en Afrique	to go on safari in Africa
faire du ski dans les Alpes	to go skiing in the Alps
chanter dans un groupe	to sing in a group
rester en bonne forme	to stay healthy
être heureux / heureuse	to be happy
faire le tour du monde	to go around the world
traverser l'Atlantique en canoë	to cross the Atlantic in a canoe

Helpful Hint

To make what you write and say about the future more interesting, you don't always have to say what you will do. You can also say what you won't do.

Je ne vais pas...	I'm not going to...
Je ne veux pas...	I don't want to...
Je ne serai pas...	I won't be...
Je n'aurai pas....	I won't have...
Je n'ai pas l'intention de (d')...	I don't intend to...

? Test Yourself

1. Practise saying each of the following phrases in French, adding your own ending to complete the sentence.

   - I would like to visit...
   - I intend to go...
   - I will live...
   - I will have...
   - I hope to work...

2. In French, make a list of 8 New Year resolutions. Make sure it includes things you won't do as well as things you will do.

   e.g. **Je vais être sympa envers mon frère.**
   I am going to be nice to my brother.
   Je ne vais pas ronger mes ongles.
   I'm not going to bite my nails.

Exam Practice

1. How long will Jean-Luc spend travelling?
2. Give two reasons why he wants to be a teacher.
3. Ultimately, what job would he like?
4. What job does Marie's father do?
5. Why does he want her to do the same?
6. Give two reasons why she does not want to do this.
7. Why is Yvette waiting to see what her grades are like?
8. What will she do in the meantime?
9. What do her parents think?

Marie - **Mon père pense que je devrais devenir vétérinaire. Il est vétérinaire et il voudrait travailler avec moi. Moi, je ne le veux pas. Les heures sont trop longues. Il faut passer quatre ans à l'université - c'est trop long. De toute façon, je ne vais pas réussir à mes examens.**

Yvette - **Je ne sais pas encore ce que je veux faire. J'attends mes résultats. En attendant, je vais trouver un placement dans un bureau. Mes parents seront d'accord parce qu'ils pensent que je devrais faire mes propres décisions.**

Jean-Luc - **Je vais voyager pour un an avant de commencer mes études universitaires. Après l'université, je veux devenir prof parce que c'est un bon emploi et je voudrais aider des enfants à apprendre. J'enseignerai l'anglais. Enfin, je voudrais devenir principal.**

Une année sabbatique/ Gap Year

Avant de continuer mes études...
Before continuing my studies...

Je voudrais voyager un peu parce que les voyages élargissent l'esprit.
I'd like to travel a bit because travel broadens the mind.

Je veux travailler à l'étranger pour connaître une culture différente.
I want to work abroad to find out about a different culture.

Je voudrais habiter et a travailler à Paris pour six mois pour perfectionner mon français.
I would like to live and work in Paris for six months to improve my French.

Je trouverai un placement pour un an parce qu'un stage en enterprise est aussi important que les diplômes.
I will get a work placement for a year because practical experience is just as important as qualifications.

Je vais travailler pour une œuvre charitable parce que c'est une occasion pour aider les gens qui sont moins heureux que moi.
I am going to do some charity work because it is an opportunity to help people less fortunate than myself.

Socia

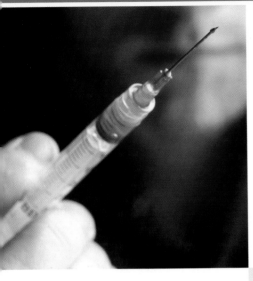

Keywords

l'alcool	alcohol	**une maladie**	illness
le tabac	tobacco	**le cancer**	cancer
la drogue	drugs	**le sida**	AIDS
un / une drogué(e)	drug addict	**la guerre**	war
un(e) toxicomane	drug addict	**la violence**	violence
la toxicomanie	drug addiction	**s'habituer à**	to get used to
une habitude	habit	**l'égalité**	equality
une annonce	advert	**le chômage**	unemployment
la publicité	advertising	**la pauvreté**	poverty
une image	image	**les sans domicile fixe (SDF)**	the homeless (with a fixed address)

La drogue et l'alcool / Drugs and alcohol

La drogue et l'alcool sont de grands problèmes parmi les jeunes.
Drugs and alcohol are big problems amongst young people.

On risque de devenir dépendant.
You risk becoming addicted.

Certaines drogues provoquent des maladies et la mort.
Some drugs cause illness and death.

Quelques jeunes volent des choses pour acheter de la drogue.
Some young people steal things to buy drugs.

L'alcool mène souvent à la violence.
Alcohol often leads to violence.

Il est dangereux de conduire après avoir bu. Cela cause des accidents de route.
It's dangerous to drive after drinking. It causes road accidents.

L'alcool provoque des maladies de foie et des crises cardiaques.
Alcohol causes liver disease and heart attacks.

Les jeunes boivent trop d'alcool. C'est pour être sociable et pour faire comme les autres.
Young people drink too much. It's to be sociable and to copy others.

Exam Practice

Le Monde

Dehors dans le froid

Je suis sans domicile fixe depuis deux ans. Je passe le temps dans la rue et je demande de l'argent aux passants. C'est monotone et triste. Le soir, souvent, je n'ai rien à manger. De temps en temps, les oeuvres charitables me donnent des vêtements et de la soupe. Le plus difficile, c'est l'hiver quand il fait froid et il pleut beaucoup.

Une journée typique d'un jeune chômeur

Je me lève à dix heures, ce n'est pas la peine de me lever plus tôt. Je ne travaille pas depuis deux ans. Je lis les annonces dans les journaux tous les jours pour les offres d'emploi. Ma vie est très ennuyeuse et monotone. Je n'ai pas beaucoup d'argent. Il est difficile d'acheter de quoi manger.

Read these firsthand accounts, written for a newspaper article, about unemployment and homelessness.

Une journée typique d'un jeune chômeur
1 How long has this person been out of work?
2 What do they do to try and find work?
3 Why is it difficult to buy things to eat?

Dehors dans le froid
4 How long has this person been homeless?
5 What does he do during the day?
6 What two things do charities provide?

Issues and Choices

Grammaire (The Pluperfect Tense)

The *pluperfect* tense is a form of past tense. It is used when you are talking about an action that happened in the past, and want to mention something that happened even earlier (i.e. preceding it). It is formed using **avoir** or **être** in the *imperfect tense*, followed by the *past participle* of the verb. In other words, it follows the same rules as the *perfect tense* (pages 13, 32, 33), but uses the *imperfect* of **avoir** and **être** instead of the present.

e.g. **J'ai commencé à boire après que mon père était parti.**
    I started drinking after my father had left.

J'ai commencé (I started) is in the perfect tense because it is a past action that is complete. Mon père était parti (my father *had* left) is in the pluperfect tense because it happened before the other action.

Here is the pluperfect form of an **avoir** verb and an **être** verb in full:

avoir:		
	J'avais commencé	I had started
	Tu avais commencé	You had started
	Il / Elle avait commencé	He / She had started
	Nous avions commencé	We had started
	Vous aviez commencé	You had started
	Ils / Elles avaient commencé	They had started

être:		
	J'étais parti(e)	I had departed
	Tu étais parti(e)	You had departed
	Il était parti	He had departed
	Elle était partie	She had departed
	Nous étions parti(s)(es)	We had departed
	Vous étiez parti(e)(s)(es)	You had departed
	Ils étaient partis	They had departed
	Elles étaient parties	They had departed

Les situations familiales / Family circumstances

Mes parents sont divorcés.
My parents are divorced.

Mes parents se séparent.
My parents are separating.

J'habite avec ma mère.
I live with my mother.

J'ai des demi-frères et demi-soeurs.
I have half-brothers and half-sisters.

Je ne m'entends pas bien avec mon beau-père.
I don't get on with my step-father.

Je vois rarement mon père.
I don't see my father very often.

Je pars en vacances deux fois par an.
I get to go on holiday twice a year.

Je reçois plus de cadeaux pour mon anniversaire.
I get more birthday presents.

 Task

Complete each sentence by choosing a pluperfect expression:

1. **Le patron a offert un emploi à Sylvie, mais…**
2. **Avant de quitter l'école…**
3. **Je suis allé à l'hôpital avec mon ami, parce qu'…**
4. **J'ai acheté des cigarettes pour mon ami, mais…**
5. **J'ai dû aller chez le dentiste parce que…**

A. **…il avait décidé d'arrêter de fumer.**
B. **…elle avait déjà trouvé un travail.**
C. **…Marcel avait décidé de ne pas aller à l'université.**
D. **…j'avais mangé trop de choses sucrées.**
E. **…il avait bu trop d'alcool.**

💡 Helpful Hint

In French, you use the phrase **avant de** to say *before* doing something. Remember to use **avant d'** in front of verbs that begin with vowels.

avant de manger before eating
avant d'arriver before arriving

Reflexive verbs need the correct pronoun:

e.g. **Avant de me lever, j'ai bu une tasse de thé.**
Before getting up I had a cup of tea.
Avant de se lever il a bu une tasse de thé.
Before getting up he had a cup of tea.

It is a bit more complicated if you want to say *after* doing something.

après avoir mangé after eating
après avoir fini after finishing
après être arrivé(e) after arriving

Again take care with reflexive verbs:

e.g. **Après m'être levé(e), je suis allé(e) dans la salle de bains.**
After getting up, I went to the bath room.
Après s'être levée, elle est allée dans la salle de bains.
After getting up she went to the bathroom.

❓ Test Yourself

In French, list three issues that concern you. For each one give a reason why.

e.g. **C'est l'avenir de notre planète qui m'inquiète le plus.**
It is the future of our planet that worries me most.
Les usines mettent des déchets dans les rivières. Cela empoisonne notre eau.
Factories put waste into the rivers. It is poisoning our water.

Les Soucis / Concerns

Je me sens concerné(e) par... I am concerned about...	**la guerre / le terrorisme / la violence / l'insécurité / la pauvreté / la famine / le racisme / les sans-abri.** war / terrorism / violence / crime / poverty / famine / racism / the homeless.
parce que / qu' ... because...	**les gens innocents sont tués.** innocent people are killed. **la violence ne résout rien.** violence solves nothing. **les gens meurent de faim en Afrique.** people die of hunger in Africa. **les gens ne se sentent pas sûrs.** people don't feel safe. **on achète des choses dont on n'a pas besoin.** we buy things we don't need. **il y a beaucoup de discrimination contre les immigrés.** there's a lot of discrimination against immigrants.
Ça me rend... It makes me feel...	**malade / dégoûté(e) / enragé(e) / impuissant(e) / triste / déprimé(e) / inquiet (inquiète) / anxieux (anxieuse).** sick / disgusted / angry / powerless / sad / depressed / worried / anxious.

La publicité / Advertising

Pour moi, il y a trop de publicité. On la voit partout, dans la rue, à la télé, dans les magazines. La publicité encourage les jeunes à acheter les choses inutiles et elle donne une impression fausse de la vie. La publicité aussi exploite les gens.
For me, there is too much advertising. One sees it everywhere, in the street, on the TV, in magazines. Advertising encourages young people to buy useless things and it gives a false impression of life. Advertising also exploits people.

Issues and Choices

Exam Practice

Read the problem page letters.

1. Who was a victim of racism?
2. When did this happen?
3. Who has just started a new school?
4. What do they ask if they should do to help make new friends?
5. Whose boss discriminates against women?
6. What does he think women should do?

Laurence, 14 ans.
J'ai commencé à une nouvelle école et c'est difficile de faire des amis. Les élèves dans ma classe ne me parlent pas. J'aime le rock, mais eux ils aiment le hip-hop et ils portent des jeans larges et des baskets. Est-ce que je devrais porter le même genre de vêtements pour être accepté?

Simone, 16 ans.
Mon patron ne me parle jamais parce qu'il croit que les femmes doivent rester à la maison pour s'occuper des enfants. Il donne à mes collègues-hommes tout le travail le plus intéressant et je dois faire le thé. Qu'est-ce qu'il faut faire pour l'encourager à me prendre au sérieux?

Elise, 15 ans.
En France, le racisme est un grand problèm. Ma meilleure copine est noire. La dernière fois que j'ai fait du shopping avec ma copine, elle a essayé d'aider une dame âgée avec ses sacs. Et la dame lui a dit: «J'ai pas besoin de l'aide d'une Arabe.» J'étais très choquée d'entendre ces mots. Pourquoi est-ce que les gens sont si racistes?

La publicité est assez amusante et j'aime regarder les publicités pour les nouveaux produits. Mais c'est aussi ennuyeux, surtout au cinéma. Je n'aime pas la publicité destinée aux enfants parce qu'ils sont trop jeunes pour comprendre.
Advertising is quite amusing and I like to see adverts for new products. But it is also boring, especially at the cinema. I do not like adverts intended for children because they are too young to understand.

Souvent la publicité est très utile, parce que cela informe les consommateurs. Beaucoup de gens travaillent dans la publicité et c'est bon pour l'économie.
Often advertising is very useful, because it informs consumers. Many people work in advertising and it is good for the economy.

Some information about grammar was included alongside the keywords and useful phrases in the main section of this revision guide, to help you understand, talk and write about the topics on those pages. The following grammar points are just as important and will help you in all areas of your GCSE French course. Make sure you learn them!

Verbs which take être in the perfect tense

Here is a complete list of *verbs* which need **être** to form the perfect tense:

aller	to go
je suis allé(e)	I went
arriver	to arrive
je suis arrivé(e)	I arrived
descendre	to go down
je suis descendu(e)	I went down
devenir	to become
je suis devenu(e)	I became
entrer	to enter
je suis entré(e)	I entered
monter	to go up
je suis monté(e)	I went up
mourir	to die
il / elle est mort(e)	he died / she died
naître	to be born
je suis né(e)	I was born
partir	to depart / leave / set off
je suis parti(e)	I left
rentrer	to go home
je suis rentré(e)	I came home
rester	to stay
je suis resté(e)	I stayed
retourner	to return
je suis retourné(e)	I returned
revenir	to come back
je suis revenu(e)	I came back
sortir	to go out
je suis sorti(e)	I went out
tomber	to fall
je suis tombé(e)	I fell
venir	to come
je suis venu(e)	I came

Adverbs

Adverbs are descriptive words that provide more information about verbs or adjectives e.g. how, where, when etc. They do not have to agree with the subject like adjectives do:

e.g. **un homme gentil**   a kind man

un homme is the noun and subject and **gentil** is the adjective. The adjective is in the masculine form to agree with the subject.

e.g. **une femme** vraiment **gentille**   a *really* kind woman

une femme is the noun and subject, **gentille** is the adjective and **vraiment** is the adverb. The adjective is in the feminine form to agree with the subject. In this case the adverb quantifies the adjective - it tells us 'how' kind the woman is. It does not have to agree with the subject.

To form many adverbs in French you take the feminine form of the adjective and add **-ment**:

e.g. **heureux**	happy
heureuse (feminine)	happy
heureusement (adverb)	happily / fortunately
doux	gentle / soft
douce (feminine)	gentle / soft
doucement (adverb)	gently / softly

If the adjective ends in a vowel, you just add **-ment**:

e.g. **vrai**	true
vraiment (adverb)	truly / really

However, not all French adverbs end in **-ment**:

e.g. **vite**	quickly
(although **rapidement** means rapidly / quickly as well)	
soudain	suddenly

Nouns in the plural

Most *nouns* take an **-s** to form the plural:

e.g. **un chat**	**deux chats**
une semaine	**trois semaines**

Nouns that end in **-eau** or **-eu** usually use an **-x** to form the plural:

e.g. **un gâteau**	**des gâteaux**
un château	**beaucoup de châteaux**

Nouns that end in **-al** usually change to **-aux** in the plural:

e.g. **un cheval**	**deux chevaux**
un journal	**les journaux**

There is one common noun that does not follow these rules:

e.g. **un œil**	an eye
les yeux	the eyes

Additional Grammar

Infinitives and Present Participles

The *infinitive* is the form of the verb that you will find in a dictionary. On its own, it normally means *to...* e.g. **chanter** means *to sing* and **manger** means *to eat*. In French, the infinitive tends to be used more often than in English:

e.g. **J'aime** chanter — I like singing
avant de manger — before eating
sans parler — without speaking

Where two verbs are used together, the second verb is often in the infinitive. Certain verbs are followed directly by the infinitive, such as verbs used to express preferences e.g. liking, disliking, wanting:

e.g. **J'adore** danser — I love dancing
Je déteste nager — I hate swimming
Je veux rentrer **à la maison** — I want to go home

Other verbs that are followed directly by the infinitive include **pouvoir** (to be able), **devoir** (to have to), **aller** (to go), **espérer** (to hope). Some verbs need **à** before the infinitive:

e.g. **Il m'a** aidé à **faire mes devoirs** — He helped me to do my homework
Il a commencé à **conduire** — He started driving

Other examples include **hésiter à** (to hesitate) and **réussir à** (to succeed). Some verbs need **de** before the infinitive:

e.g. **Elle a** fini de **manger** — She has finished eating
J'ai cessé de **fumer** — I have given up smoking
Nous avons décidé de **partir** — We decided to go

Other examples include **essayer de** (to try) and **avoir l'intention de** (to intend). All prepositions are followed by the infinitive (except **en**):

e.g. **Je suis allé au cinéma** pour **voir un film d'horreur**
I went to the cinema to see a horror film

The preposition **en** is followed by a part of the verb called the *present participle*. This is formed by taking the **nous** form of the present tense (e.g. **nous** regardons, **nous** finissons, **nous** faisons), removing the **-ons** ending and replacing it with **-ant**.

e.g. **Regard**ons becomes **regard**ant
Finissons becomes **finiss**ant
Faisons becomes **fais**ant

en + *present participle* can mean *in* doing something, *on* doing something, *while* doing something or *by* doing something:

e.g. **Il a fait une bonne chose** en aidant **son ami**
He did a good thing *in helping* his friend
En arrivant, **j'ai défait ma valise**
On arriving I unpacked my suitcase
Je mange en regardant **la télé**
I eat *while watching* the TV
Il se relaxe en écoutant **la musique**
He relaxes *by listening* to music

The Subjunctive

Although you are not expected to be able to use the *subjunctive* yourself, you may occasionally come across it in written and spoken French. The subjunctive is a special form of the verb that is often used after conjunctions such as:

bien que — although
pourvu que — provided that
à moins que — unless
pour que — so that

Here are some common verbs in the subjunctive:

e.g. **Je vais sortir bien qu'**il fasse **froid** (from **faire**)
I'm going out even though it is cold.

Je vais faire du ski bien que ce soit **cher** (from **être**)
I'm going skiing although it is dear.

Il viendra pourvu qu'il ait **le temps** (from **avoir**)
He'll come provided he has the time.

Elle a changé la date pour que tu puisses **venir** (from **pouvoir**)
She's changed the date so that you can come.

Pronouns

Pronouns are useful words, which prevent us from having to repeat ourselves:

e.g. **J'adore les frites. Je les mange tous les jours.**
     I love chips. I eat *them* every day.

The problem in French is knowing which pronoun to use and where to put it in the sentence. The following are known as *direct pronouns*:

me (or **m'**)	me	**nous**	us	**le** (or **l'**)	him/it
te (or **t'**)/**vous**	you	**les**	them	**la** (or **l'**)	her/it

Direct pronouns go in front of the verb (use **m'**, **t'** or **l'** before a verb that starts with a vowel):

e.g. **Il me déteste**   He hates me
     Il la regarde   He's watching her
     Il le voit souvent   He often sees him

In the *perfect tense* (see pages 13, 32, 33), the direct pronoun comes in front of **avoir**. If it is feminine or plural, it makes the past participle agree.

e.g. **J'ai mangé un croissant**   I ate a croissant
     Je l'ai mangé   I ate *it*
     J'ai mangé une pomme   I ate an apple
     Je l'ai mangée   I ate *it*
     J'ai mangé des chips   I ate some crisps
     Je les ai mangés   I ate *them*
     J'ai mangé des frites   I ate some chips
     Je les ai mangées   I ate *them*

Verbs which are followed by à e.g. **parler à** (to talk to), **donner à** (to give to), **demander à** (to ask), **dire à** (to say/tell) require an *indirect pronoun*.

The *indirect pronouns* are the same as the *direct pronouns*, with the exception of **le/la** which become **lui,** and **les** which becomes **leur.** They still go before the verb, but do not make the past participle agree in the perfect tense.

e.g. **Il me parle**   He talks to *me*
     Il lui demande de l'argent   He's asking *him* for money
     Il leur a donné un cadeau   He gave *them* a present

When used with an imperative (in a command), the pronoun comes after the verb. Note that after the imperative you use **moi** (instead of **me**) and **toi** (instead of **te**):

e.g. **Donnez-le-moi**   give *it* to me

Other useful pronouns: **Y** means *there* and **En** can mean *of it, of them* or *some*:

e.g. **J'aime la France. J'y vais tous les ans.**
     I love France. I go *there* every year.
     Mon école est à cinq minutes de chez moi. J'y vais à pied.
     My school is 5 minutes from my house. I go *there* on foot.
     Tu as des pommes? Oui j'en ai deux.
     Have you any apples. Yes I have two *of them*.

Qui and **que** are *relative pronouns*. **Qui** is followed by a verb and is used to talk about the *subject* of the verb. It can refer to people or objects.

e.g. **J'ai un frère qui s'appelle Pierre.**
     I have a brother who is called Pierre.
     (**un frère** is the subject of the verb **appeler**)

e.g. **J'habite à Manchester qui se trouve dans le nord-ouest de l'Angleterre.**
     I live in Manchester which is situated in the north west of England.
     (**Manchester** is the subject of the verb **trouver**)

Que is the *object* of the verb i.e. it is used when the action of the verb is happening to someone/something else. Again, it can refer to people or objects.

e.g. **J'ai parlé à la jeune fille que tu aimes.**
     I've spoken to the girl (*whom*) you fancy.
     (**tu** is the subject of the verb **aimer** and **la jeune fille** is the object)

e.g. **J'ai perdu le stylo que ma mère m'a offert.**
     I've lost the pen *which* my mother gave me.
     (**ma mère** is the subject of the verb **offrir** and **le stylo** is the object)

When **que** is used in conjunction with **de** it becomes **dont**

e.g. **J'ai besoin d'un stylo. Tu as le stylo dont j'ai besoin.**
     I need a pen. You've got the pen *which* I need.

Dont can also be used to mean *whose*.

e.g. **Voici le garçon dont je connais la mère.**
     There's the boy *whose* mother I know.

Additional Grammar

Lequel (masculine singular), **laquelle** (feminine singular), **lesquels** (masculine plural) and **lesquelles** (feminine plural) are known as *interrogative pronouns* i.e. they are used in questions.

e.g. **Lequel des professeurs est le meilleur?**
Which of the teachers is the best?

Laquelle des jupes préfères-tu?
Which of the skirts do you prefer?

In answer to these questions you can use a *demonstrative pronoun*: **celui** (masculine singular), **celle** (feminine singular), **ceux** (masculine plural) and **celles** (feminine plural).

e.g. **Je préfère celui qui enseigne le français.**
I prefer *the one* who teaches French.

J'aime mieux celle qui est plus courte que les autres.
I prefer *the one* which is shorter than the others.

Possessive pronouns are used to tell you who owns something.

- **C'est à qui, ce pullover?**   Whose is this pullover?
  C'est le mien.   It's mine. (masculine singular)
- **C'est à qui, cette écharpe?**   Whose is this scarf?
  C'est la mienne.   It's mine. (feminine singular)
- **C'est à qui, ces gants?**   Whose are these gloves?
  Ce sont les miens.   They're mine. (masculine plural)
- **C'est à qui, ces lunettes?**   Whose are these glasses?
  Ce sont les miennes.   They're mine. (feminine plural)

Other examples include...

le tien, la tienne, les tiens, les tiennes	Yours
le sien, la sienne, les siens, les siennes	His/hers
le nôtre, la nôtre, les nôtres (m/f plural)	Ours
le vôtre, la vôtre, les vôtres (m/f plural)	Yours
le leur, la leur, les leurs (m/f plural)	Theirs

Other useful words:

- **Chaque**   every
  Chaque année, on va en Espagne.   Every year, we go to Spain.
- **Chacun/chacune**   each one/every one
  Chacune des filles a un livre.   Every one of the girls has a book.
- **Quelque/quelques**   some/several
  Quelques jours plus tard   Several days later
- **Quelqu'un**   someone
  Quelqu'un a pris mon sac.   Someone's taken my bag.

The Passive

Normally the action of the verb is carried out by the subject. The *passive* voice occurs when someone/something else (not necessarily mentioned) carries out the action i.e. the subject is *acted upon*. In French, as in English, the passive is formed when the verb *to be* (**être**) is used with the past participle. The past participle must agree with the subject.

e.g. **Les parents sont consultés**
The parents *are consulted*
(**Les Parents** is the subject and **consulter** is the verb acting upon it.)

The passive can often be avoided using the pronoun *on*:

e.g. **On consulte les parents**
One/Someone *consults* the parents
(**On** becomes the subject of the verb **consulter** and **les parents** becomes the object.)

The passive is formed in the same way regardless of the tense:

Imperfect
les parents étaient consultés
The parents *were consulted*

Perfect
ma maison a été cambriolée
My house *was burgled*

Future
la chambre sera nettoyée
The room *will be cleaned*

A

In addition to the vocabulary covered in the main section of this guide (pages 6-85), you could come across any of the following words in a reading or listening test, so make sure you learn them. You might find them useful when writing and speaking French too!

(en) avance	(in) advance	**un département**	a county
à l'étranger	abroad	**un dépliant**	a leaflet
à part	a part	**un dessert**	a dessert/sweet
accepter	to accept	**un dialogue**	a dialogue/conversation
l'ambiance (f)	atmosphere	**distribuer**	to distribute
amicalement	best wishes	**la douane**	customs
un apprentissage	an apprenticeship		(e.g. at the airport)
attendre	to wait	**un drapeau**	a flag
un bal	a ball (e.g. a dance)	**empêcher**	to prevent
un baladeur	a walkman	**un emploi**	a job
une balle	a ball (tennis)	**en plein air**	outdoors
un ballon	a ball (football)	**l'entraînement (m)**	training/coaching
une barbe	a beard	**une enveloppe**	an envelope
un bateau	a boat	**une épaule**	a shoulder
un biscuit	a cake/biscuit	**un épicier**	a grocer
un bol	a bowl	**des espaces (m)**	spaces
une brochure	a brochure/leaflet	**une excursion**	a trip/excursion
		la fac	university (**la faculté**)
un bureau de renseignements	a information office		
		faire dans la vie	to do for a living
		(e.g. **que fait ton perè dans la vie!**)	
un cadeau	a gift/present		
une cassette	a cassette tape	**la farine**	flour
certainement	certainly	**le feu**	fire/light
un champ	a field	**frapper**	to hit/strike
châtain	chestnut brown	**un gant**	a glove
le chômage	unemployment	**gras**	fat
le ciel	the sky	**un groupe**	a group
la circulation	circulation/traffic	**l'hospitalité (f)**	hospitality
un club	a club	**l'huile (f)**	oil
un coin	a corner	**le jogging**	jogging
une colline	a hill	**un laboratoire**	a laboratory
un commerce	a business/commerce	**une leçon**	a lesson
un concours	a competition	**une liste**	a list
un conducteur	a driver	**local**	local
connaître	to know	**une machine**	a machine
copier	to copy/reproduce	**un magazine**	a magazine
le danger	danger/risk	**malheureusement**	unfortunately
de la part de qui	on behalf of	**le marketing**	marketing
déménager	to move house	**le match**	match/game

litional Vocabulary

mixte	mixed / combined	**une partie**	a part
la mode	fashion	**du pâté (m)**	pâté
une montre	a watch	**le péage**	toll
montrer	to show	**un pique-nique**	a picnic
la mort	death	**pleurer**	to cry
un mouton	a sheep	**un policier**	a policeman
la naissance	birth	**un pont**	a bridge
un oignon	an onion	**un portière**	a door (of car)
un orchestre	an orchestra	**présenter**	to introduce
le parfum	flavour	**prêt**	ready
un partenaire	a partner		

proposer	to propose / suggest
la queue	tail / queue
une raison	a reason
la réaction	reaction
recommander	recommend
regretter	to regret / be sorry
remercier	to thank
un réservation	a reservation
la responsabilité	responsibility / reliability
rire	to laugh / smile / joke
une rivière	a river
s' entraîner	to train (e.g. for a sport)
s'approcher	to approach
le sable	sand
le salaire	salary
sans travail	out of work / unemployed
sauter	to jump
se reposer	to rest
un séjour	a stay / visit / stopover
le shopping	shopping
si on allait…?	should we go…?
les sports d'hiver (m)	winter sports
une surprise	a surprise
le syndicat d'initiative	tourist information office
du toast (m)	toast
les toilettes (f)	toilets
le tourisme	tourism
le touriste	tourist
tout le monde	everyone
un trajet	a journey
une trousse	a pencil case
une vache	a cow
valable	valid
la vanille	vanilla
varié	varied / various
le veau	calf / veal
vérifier	check (e.g. tickets)
le vinaigre	vinegar
le visage	face
visiter	to visit
une vitamine	a vitamin
vivre	to live
une voie	a way / route
le voile	sailing
la vue	view

Writing

Dictionaries

You are not allowed to use a dictionary in a written examination. You can use a dictionary for coursework, however, you should only use it to check spellings and genders. Don't look up new words, which you may get wrong.

The Golden Rule

If you don't know a word in French, don't use it. Think of an alternative instead. For example, if you are asked to list 4 school subjects in an exam, don't guess at words. Stick to the ones you are sure about and know how to spell e.g. **les maths**, **le sport**, **les sciences**, **l'anglais**.

Four Tips for Longer Written Pieces

1 Use adjectives and adverbs whenever possible.

e.g. **J'ai visité un** grand **parc d'attractions** intéressant. **C'était** très **amusant.**

You can also use **assez** (fairly/quite), **trop** (too), **un peu** (a bit) to make your description more interesting.

2 Demonstrate a good range of past and future tenses. Here are some common ones:

Past

Je suis allé(e)…	I went…	**On est allé…**	We went…
J'ai visité…	I visited…	**On a visité…**	We visited…
J'ai mangé…	I ate…	**On a mangé…**	We ate…
J'ai acheté…	I bought…	**On a acheté…**	We bought…
Je suis resté(e)…	I stayed…	**On est resté…**	We stayed…
J'étais…	I was…	**C'était…**	It was…

Future

Je voudrais visiter…	I'd like to visit…
Je veux acheter…	I want to buy…
Je vais aller…	I'm going to go…
J'espère habiter…	I hope to live…
J'irai…	I'll go…
Je serai…	I'll be…
J'aurai…	I'll have…
Ce sera…	It will be…
J'ai l'intention de travailler…	I intend to work…

3 Include as many personal opinions as possible.

A mon avis, c'était…	In my opinion it was…
Je l'ai trouvé…	I thought it was…
Je pense que c'est…	I think it's…
Je crois que ce sera…	I believe it will be…

4 Use connectives to make your sentences longer.

Le voyage était long et **fatigant.**
Le musée était grand mais **intéressant.**
J'ai visité une ville qui **s'appelle…**
Je suis allé au cinéma où **j'ai vu une comédie** qui **s'appelle…**
J'adore jouer au foot parce que **c'est très amusant** et aussi **c'est bon pour la santé.**
J'aime faire de la natation donc **je suis allée à la piscine.**

Exam Advice

 Listening

Four Tips for Listening Tests

1 Use the 5 minute preparation time sensibly. Look at the context of the questions (e.g. if the question is about school, you know you will be hearing information about school related subjects). For multiple choice questions, read all the possible answers and listen out for keywords and phrases.

2 Do not panic if you don't understand everything on the tape. You will hear everything twice and many people find they understand more as the test goes on and they get used to the sound of the spoken French. Make a note of everything you *do* understand. This information might help you to make sense of what you have heard and answer the question. For example…

A typical listening question might ask you to correctly match three people with their personal interests. On the paper there would be 4 symbols representing gardening, cooking, music and playing cards and on the tape you would hear:

> **Personne 1: J'aime bien jouer aux cartes avec mes amies.**
> **Personne 2: J'adore jouer du piano. La musique, c'est ma passion.**
> **Personne 3: J'aime beaucoup faire la cuisine. Ma spécialité, c'est le gâteau au chocolat.**

Personne 1: you might only understand the word **amies.** If so, make a note of it.

Personne 2: you might find this one quite easy to understand and choose the *music* symbol. (This cuts down the number of possible choices for the other questions).

Personne 3: you might recognise the words **gâteau** and **chocolat**, so you would choose the *cooking* symbol.

You are now left with two symbols. The word **amies** suggests that Personne 1 is talking about something you can do with friends. This means that *playing cards* is most likely to be the answer.

3 Try to visualise words. Words which would be easy to understand in a reading test (e.g. **théâtre**, **athlétisme**, **train**) are often harder to understand in a listening test. As you listen to the tape, try to visualise how the words look in French. This can help you to understand their meaning.

4 Listen out for negatives. Negatives can often change the whole meaning of a passage, so listen out for them. This is particularly important in higher tier tests. Here are the most common examples:

Ne…pas	**Je ne vais pas au cinéma**
	I *don't* go to the cinema
Ne…jamais	**Je ne vais jamais au supermarché**
	I *never* go to the supermarket
Ne…plus	**Je ne vais plus à la piscine**
	I don't go to the pool *any more*
Ne…rien	**Je ne mange rien le soir**
	I don't eat *anything* in the evening
Ne…personne	**Je ne vois personne**
	I can't see *anybody*

Dictionaries

Dictionaries are not allowed for listening tests, but you will be given 5 minutes preparation time before the tape starts.

The Golden Rule

Listening tests often include a lot of multiple choice questions. Make sure your letters are clearly formed and never leave a blank space. If a question is in French, answer it in French; if the question is in English, answer in English.

Reading

Dictionaries

Dictionaries are not allowed for reading tests.

The Golden Rule

Reading tests often incorporate a lot of multiple choice questions. Make sure your letters are clearly formed and never leave a blank space. If a question is given in French, answer it in French. If the question is in English, answer it in English. They are also likely to include questions where you must answer *true*, *false* or *not mentioned*. Look for keywords and phrases and use *not mentioned* sparingly!

Four Tips for Reading

1 Learn lots of synonyms. Synonyms are words that mean the same (or nearly the same) thing. Many reading questions feature these.

A typical question might ask you to identify someone's hobbies. The text might read: **J'adore aller à la piscine et je fais de l'équitation le week-end. Quand je reste à la maison, j'aime lire des romans.**

A faire du cheval
B la gymnastique
C la natation
D le football
E la lecture

The correct answers would be **A** (**cheval** means *horse* and **equitation** means *horse-riding*), **C** (**natation** means *swimming* and **piscine** means *swimming pool*) and **E** (**lire** means *to read* and **la lecture** means *reading*).

2 Watch out for **faux amis**. **Faux amis** (false friends) are French words that look the same as English words, but have a different meaning, like **la lecture** above. Other common ones are:

la serviette	towel
le car	coach
la journée	day
travailler	to work

3 Make sure you recognise the interrogatives. Interrogatives are questioning words. You might be asked some questions in French, so make sure you can recognise them:

Qui?	Who?
Que?	What?
Qu'est-ce que...?	What...? (when followed by a verb)
Pourquoi?	Why?
Comment?	How? (or *describe* e.g. **comment est la maison?**)
Où?	Where?
Combien?	How much/how many?
Combien de temps?	How long?
Quand?	When?
Quel?	Which? (or *what* when used before a noun e.g. **Quel temps fait-il?** And depending on whether the noun is masculine, feminine, singular or plural, you will see either **quel**, **quelle**, **quels** or **quelles**)

4 Pay attention to context. Looking at the context in which they occur, you can use your knowledge to work out the meaning of unfamiliar words.

e.g. **Je m'intéresse à la photographie et pour Noël, mes parents m'ont offert un nouvel appareil.**

You may not recognise the word **appareil**, but if you understand **photographie**, **Noël**, and **parents** you could potentially work out that the person likes photography and, for Christmas, his parents gave him a ...*camera* (**un appareil**).

Exam Advice

 **Speaking**

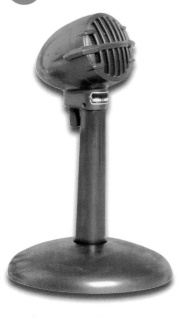

Dictionaries

You are not allowed to refer to a dictionary during a speaking test. As part of the course you will be asked to give a presentation, which will be recorded on audio cassette. You are allowed notes for this but you cannot read aloud from a script.

The Golden Rule

Say as much as you can and avoid one word answers like *yes* and *no*. Although you will be marked on pronunciation and accuracy, communication is the most important thing. Don't worry about making mistakes - this is your chance to show what you know. There will be no trick questions and the role plays and conversations you are asked to take part in will be on topics that appear on the course specification. Make sure you have something ready to say on all the major topics covered in this revision guide e.g. personal information, school, hobbies, holidays, work and pocket money, environment, health, daily routine etc.

Four Tips for Speaking Tests

1 Use the preparation time sensibly. Before the test starts you will be given some preparation time. Use this to decide what you are going to say in the role play. At foundation tier, the instructions are in English, but at higher tier, they are in French. Higher tier students should be prepared for the teacher/examiner to ask a question that is not on the card. A good knowledge of the *interrogative* forms (see the reading section, opposite) should help you to understand what you are being asked.

2 Anticipate questions. Try to take the initiative and anticipate what follow-up questions you might be asked. This will help you to give longer answers and provide the teacher/examiner with the information they are looking for. For example, if you are asked about your favourite school subject (**Quelle est ta matière préférée?**), don't just give a one word answer. Say what you like and why. You can mention other subjects that you like and even some that you don't like.

> e.g. **Je préfère l'histoire parce que c'est intéressant. J'adore aussi l'anglais – le prof est sympa. Je n'aime pas les maths parce que c'est barbant et le prof est strict.**

3 Use different tenses where appropriate. You need to demonstrate that you can use and understand different tenses (see the writing section, page 92). Have a few sentences prepared that can be adapted to suit any topic:

Past tense

Le week-end dernier je suis allé au cinéma **avec mes amis pour** regarder un film qui s'appelle Happy Jack. **C'était** amusant**...** (Hobbies)

Le week-end dernier je suis allé au centre sportif **avec mes amis pour** jouer au badminton. **C''était** amusant mais fatigant**...** (Health)

Le week-end dernier je suis allé au centre commercial **avec mes amis pour** acheter des vêtements. **C''était** ennuyeaux**...** (Shopping/Money)

Future plans

A l'avenir, je voudrais aller à l'université **pour** étudier les maths **parce que** je veux travailler dans un banque**...** (Education/Work)

A l'avenir, je voudrais aller en Italie **pour** visiter Rome **parce que** je veux voir les ruines romaines**...** (Holidays/Travel)

A l'avenir, je voudrais aller au centre sportif **pour** faire de la gymnastique **parce que** je veux rester en forme**...** (Hobbies/Health)

4 Include lots of personal opinions. Again, it is important to include as many relevant personal opinions as possible. The following phrases are invaluable when it comes to expressing your point of view:

A mon avis, c'est...	In my opinion it's...
Je l'ai trouvé...	I thought it was...
Je pensais que c'était...	I thought it was...
Je crois que ce sera...	I believe it will be...